A LIGHT FOR MY PATH

A Light for My Path

Meeting God in 365 Key Chapters of the Bible

Kenneth and Karen Boa

SERVANT PUBLICATIONS
ANN ARBOR, MICHIGAN

Vine Books is an imprint of Servant Publications especially designed to serve evangelical Christians.

Scripture quotations from the New American Standard Bible, Copyright 1960, 1962, 1963, 1968, 1971, 1972, 1973, 1975, 1977, 1995 by The Lockman Foundation.

Published by Servant Publications
P.O. Box 8617
Ann Arbor, Michigan 48107

Cover design by Eric Walljasper–Minneapolis, MN

01 02 03 04 10 9 8 7 6 5 4 3 2 1

Printed in the United States of America
ISBN 1–56955–258–4

Library of Congress Cataloging–in–Publication Data

Boa, Kenneth
   A light for my path : meeting God in 365 key chapters of the Bible / Kenneth Boa.
      p. cm.
   ISBN 1–56955–258–4 (alk. paper)
    1. Bible–Meditations. 2. Devotional calendars. I. Title.

BS491 .5 B62 2001
242'.5–dc21

2001026207

Introduction

The Purpose of This Book

Many people would love to know the Bible and to understand the beauty and flow of its literary narratives and interwoven themes. Due to its sheer size and structural complexity, however, grasping the message of the Bible can be a daunting task. Often when people decide to join the tiny minority of people who have actually read the Scriptures from Genesis to Revelation, they get bogged down by the time they reach the books of Leviticus or Deuteronomy. The few who press on through the historical books wonder what happened to the story line when they arrive at the poets and prophets. The multiple historical references to people, places, and events–combined with the intricacies of the narratives–make it difficult for people to put the pieces of the puzzle together in a meaningful way.

With these problems in mind, this handbook is designed to guide you through the highlights of Scripture by taking you on a tour of 365 key chapters during the course of a year. By reading the introductory material for each chapter, you will get a concise overview of the Scripture reading for that day, and this will aid you in your understanding. These daily introductions present the necessary historical backgrounds, literary flow, story line, and central issues in the chapters you will read. I selected these chapters to give you the big picture of the Bible so that by the time you have completed this tour, you will have a clear grasp of the message of Scripture.

How to Use This Book

As you can quickly see by looking at any of the 365 readings, each day has four elements: one or two brief introductory paragraphs, an invitation to read the appropriate chapter from your Bible, a prayer related to the message of the chapter, and one or more meditation verses from that day's reading.

Take your time as you read the introductory material so that it will become an aid to your understanding. For your chapter reading, use a translation of the Bible that is clear and accessible to you, or try more than one translation. (I used the updated edition of the *New American Standard Bible* for the direct Scripture quotations in this book.) Keep this book open during your Scripture reading so that you can refer at any time to the introductory comments.

After your Bible reading, be sure to read the prayer slowly and thoughtfully, and then take some time to form your own response to the Scripture chapter you have just read.

Finally, read the meditation passage for the day, and if there is more than one meditation verse in the chapter, you may want to select the passage that speaks most directly to you. Simply take a few moments to move slowly through the passage and reflect on each of the phrases and images. Consider writing this passage on an index card to carry with you throughout the day. In this way, you can review your passage by looking at the card at any time (for example, while waiting in line or at traffic lights). It is much better to meditate on truth than to meditate on negative thoughts about people or problems.

This book of the law shall not depart from your mouth, but you shall meditate on it day and night, so that you may be careful to do according to all that is written in it; for then you will make your way prosperous, and then you will have success.

JOSHUA 1:8

Whatever is true, whatever is honorable, whatever is right, whatever is pure, whatever is lovely, whatever is of good repute, if there is any excellence and if anything worthy of praise, dwell on these things.

PHILIPPIANS 4:8

Day 1—Genesis 1

Genesis, the book of beginnings, provides us with a cosmic perspective on the foundation of the heavens and the earth as well as the origins of humans, who have been created in his image and likeness. In the first three days God ordered his creation, and in the last three days he populated it. Day 1 relates to day 4, day 2 to day 5, and day 3 to day 6. At the end of the sixth day, God was pleased with his creative work and declared it "very good."

In this chapter we discover our true dignity as people who have been created by and for God as his image–bearers, and we see the extensive authority with which he entrusted us.

READ GENESIS 1

Prayer: *Lord, I am amazed at the diversity, beauty, and complexity of your creation. Heaven and earth are full of the majesty of your glory, and the created order points beyond itself to you. Give me a greater sense of wonder and awe at all that you have done. May I never take your wonderful world for granted.*

Meditation passage for today: verse 27

Day 2—Genesis 3

The climax of Genesis 1 was the creation of the man and the woman, and the climax of Genesis 2 was the covenant relationship between the man and the woman. Today's chapter is crucial to our understanding of human nature: God did not create us the way we are now. We changed ourselves through the tragedy of the Fall.

The fundamental issue in the temptation scene was whether we would trust God enough to believe that he has our best interests at heart. When the man and the woman decided that they knew their own best interests better than God did, they turned from saying "Thy will be done" to "My will be done." Spiritually separated from God, their characters and destinies were radically altered.

READ GENESIS 3

Prayer: *Lord, I realize that I have participated in this scene of rebellion against you. Like Adam and Eve, I have sought to experience life on my terms. By your grace, I acknowledge this sin of pride. Root out of me all that is contrary to your purposes and character, so that Christ may be all in all in my life.*

Meditation passage for today: verse 15

Day 3—Genesis 4

The Fall had an immediate "ripple effect." Rebellion against God's good and loving purposes distorted every relationship God had designed for us: between us and God, between us and the created order, and among ourselves.

The barrier between God and us produced internal and external conflicts. The murder of Abel by his brother Cain is a prototype of the hostility and social degeneration caused by the pride and selfishness of sin. Although the line of godly Abel was cut off, God in his mercy gave Adam and Eve another son. It would be through the godly line of Seth that the ancestors of the Messiah would spring forth.

READ GENESIS 4

Prayer: *Lord, thank you that your Word reveals not only the depth of human sin and iniquity but also the height of your love and grace. Help me to remember that sin and disobedience are always destructive, and that righteousness and obedience to you are always creative and life-giving.*

Meditation passage for today: verses 25–26

Day 4—Genesis 6

Because of the rampant spread of evil, God took radical measures to destroy the ungodly in order to preserve a tiny remnant of the godly. Since the Lord found righteousness only in Noah and his family, he instructed Noah to prepare for the universal destruction that God would bring upon the earth. In this way, earth would be renewed by the human and animal life that had been preserved through the violent waters of the Flood.

READ GENESIS 6

Prayer: *Lord, the life expectancy of people living today continues to grow. And yet, prior to the Flood, people lived for hundreds of years! Unfortunately, this longevity only increased human malevolence and wickedness. Help me to be a good steward of the time you have entrusted to me. By your grace, I will not allow sin and rebellion to fester and multiply in my thoughts, words, and deeds. Thank you for your patience and forgiveness.*

Meditation passage for today: verses 5–7

Day 5—Genesis 7

Because Noah found grace in the eyes of the Lord, God showed him how to build a stable ark that would withstand the floodwaters for a year and preserve him and his family through this devastating judgment. Noah put his faith into practice and obediently fulfilled God's instructions, though it cost him and his sons decades of toil and ridicule. Noah also obeyed God's mandate to populate the ark with two of each kind of unclean animal and seven of every type of clean animal and bird.

READ GENESIS 7

Prayer: *Lord, I am grateful for this account of your obedient servant Noah, who trusted you enough to obey you even when your instructions didn't seem to make sense. Thank you for the way this great ark typifies the grace of Christ, who delivers us from the flood of sin and death.*

Meditation passage for today: verses 5, 23

Day 6—Genesis 8

As the floodwaters receded, Noah opened the window of the ark twice to see if the land had dried out enough to leave the ark. The first time Noah sent out a raven, the second time a dove. Both birds returned to the ark, unable to find a safe place to nest. The third time Noah again sent out the dove. This time the bird did not return.

When the earth had dried, Noah obeyed God's instructions to go out of the ark and to repopulate the earth with the animals and with his own descendants. In response to Noah's burnt offerings on the altar, the Lord promised that he would never again destroy the earth through another catastrophic deluge.

READ GENESIS 8

Prayer: *Lord, I am grateful for your servant Noah and his faithfulness to your commandments. Just as we are all descended from Adam through Noah, a righteous man, may I exhibit your righteousness for future generations.*

Meditation passage for today: verses 17, 22

Day 7—Genesis 9

After the Flood, the Lord reinstated his mandate for humanity to "be fruitful and multiply, and fill the earth." He also gave Noah and his descendants both animal and plant life to eat, stipulating that flesh could not be consumed with its lifeblood.

God also established a covenant with Noah and his descendants. The rainbow became the sign of this covenant. It appears that ecological conditions on earth were radically different after the Flood. These changes in the atmosphere may have accelerated the fermentation of grape juice (which could account for the drunkenness of Noah).

READ GENESIS 9

Prayer: *Lord, thank you for your covenant relationship with Noah and for this account of your faithfulness to him and his descendants. Thank you for your faithfulness, even when the world around us is changing rapidly.*

Meditation passage for today: verses 6–7

Day 8—Genesis 11

Prior to the construction of the Tower of Babel, there was one universal language. After the Flood, God had commanded those in the ark to multiply and populate the earth. However, people resisted this, seeking to stay in one place rather than to be "scattered abroad over the face of the whole earth." By confusing their language, the Lord forced the people to obey his mandate and thwarted their arrogant attempt to attain greatness on their own terms. The sudden multiplicity of languages forced people to segregate, moving away from each other and becoming autonomous communities.

This chapter includes a genealogical line that traces the descendants of Shem to Abram, the key figure of the next portion of Genesis.

READ GENESIS 11

Prayer: *Lord, your wisdom and power are great, and your purposes stand to all generations. I am grateful that in your sovereignty, the plans of those who rebel against you actually contribute to your plan, and that your Word gives us a long-term perspective on human history.*

Meditation passage for today: verse 9

Day 9—Genesis 12

This crucial chapter records God's calling Abram, choosing him from among all the people of the earth, and the threefold outline of the Abrahamic covenant: land, seed, and blessing. God's promise to give Abram and his descendants a land and a permanent lineage is a theme found in much of the Old Testament. This covenant also affirms that in Abram, "all the families of the earth will be blessed." The name of Abraham has indeed become great; he is revered by Jews, Muslims, and Christians alike.

Abram was a man of faith who learned to recognize the voice of God, to call upon his name, and to obey him.

READ GENESIS 12

Prayer: *Lord, thank you for the faith of this man who was willing to trust you and to risk everything on your promises and commands. In spite of his lapses and shortcomings, you continued to use him, just as you desire to use me.*

Meditation passage for today: verses 1–3

Day 10—Genesis 15

This chapter is crucial to understanding Abram's relationship with the Lord, who called him out of Ur of the Chaldeans to be the father of nations. When the Lord promised that Abram's descendants would be as numerous as the stars, Abram "believed in the Lord; and he reckoned it to him as righteousness." The Lord then ratified his blood covenant with Abram and his descendants by passing between the pieces of the animals. Because Abram believed God, he was justified by grace through faith.

READ GENESIS 15

Prayer: *Lord, your faithfulness and loyal love reach to the heavens, and none of your promises ever fail. Give me the grace to trust you more and to believe your promises.*

Meditation passage for today: verses 1, 5–6

Day 11—Genesis 18

Three men appeared to Abraham and affirmed that Abraham and Sarah would become the parents of the son of the covenant promise God had made earlier. When Sarah laughed, believing that she and her husband were well past their childbearing years, the Lord responded, "Is anything too difficult for the Lord?"

One of the three men was the "angel of the Lord," evidently a manifestation of the pre-incarnate Christ, since he was called the Lord. Abraham, concerned with the righteousness and justice of God, interceded on behalf of the people of Sodom until the Lord agreed that if ten righteous people could be found there, he would not destroy the city.

READ GENESIS 18

Prayer: *Lord, nothing is too difficult for you. Your character is perfect and your ways are just, righteous, and true. Let me trust in your ways and walk in them.*

Meditation passage for today: verses 14, 19, 25

Day 12—Genesis 21

Just as the Lord had predicted, Sarah miraculously conceived and bore Isaac, the covenant son God had promised to Abraham and Sarah. This time, Sarah laughed with joy. "Who would have said to Abraham that Sarah would nurse children? Yet I have borne him a son in his old age."

Attempting to "help God," Sarah had sent her maid Hagar to Abraham to conceive the child that the Lord had promised them. This plan backfired when Isaac was born. As Isaac grew, tension also grew between Sarah and Hagar. Ultimately Hagar and her son Ishmael were sent out into the wilderness, where the Lord provided for them and preserved their lives. Meanwhile, Abraham continued to grow in faith and called on the name of the Lord, the Everlasting God.

READ GENESIS 21

Prayer: *Lord, like Abraham and Sarah, I often try to take matters into my own hands and seek to accomplish things in my own timing, way, and power. I thank you that your ways are far above my own, and I ask for the grace to trust in your ways without trying to manipulate the outcome.*

Meditation passage for today: verses 5–7, 33

Day 13—Genesis 22

Over the years of walking with the Lord, Abraham learned to trust God's voice and obey it. As his faith grew, the Lord increased the level of risk. The supreme test, recorded in this chapter, revealed through Abraham's actions all that God had accomplished in his servant's heart over the years.

For Abraham to sacrifice Isaac, the son of the covenant through whom Abraham's descendants would be named, meant that the only way the promises could be fulfilled would be for Isaac to rise from the dead (see Heb 11:19). God was pleased with Abraham's demonstration of faith and honored his obedience by providing a substitute for his son.

READ GENESIS 22

Prayer: *Lord, I am stunned at the level of trust and obedience your servant Abraham exhibited in his willingness to risk everything on your command. I ask that you would work a similar measure of trust in me. Make me willing to let loose the things that would compete with my allegiance to you.*

Meditation passage for today: verses 12, 16–18

Day 14—Genesis 24

A braham's careful instructions to his servant reveal his concern for finding God's intended bride for Isaac. He knew that he and his family had been called by the Lord to be a representative people through whom all the families of the earth would be blessed. He did not want disobedience or expedience to corrupt this godly line of destiny.

When the servant found Rebekah, she must have discerned God's hand in the arrangement, for she took a risk in going with the servant to marry Abraham's son Isaac, sight unseen.

READ GENESIS 24

Prayer: *Lord, the Scriptures affirm that when people are willing to obey you by walking out into the unknown and trusting in your guidance, you always honor their faith. Let me maintain the proper object of faith by fixing my eyes on Jesus and pursuing him with a whole heart.*

Meditation passage for today: verses 40, 48

Day 15—Genesis 27

Esau sold his birthright to his conniving brother Jacob for a bowl of stew. In this chapter, the supplanter deceives his father Isaac to obtain Esau's blessing as well. Rebekah encouraged her favorite son to do this, thinking that God's promise that "the older shall serve the younger" (Gn 25:23) would be fulfilled. The plot worked but not in the way they thought. Jacob succeeded in gaining his brother's blessing, but he had to flee for his life and live for decades away from his country. Rebekah experienced the unexpected sorrow of never seeing her son Jacob again.

READ GENESIS 27

Prayer: *Lord, your Word reveals the consequences of deception, even with the best of intentions. Guard my steps from manipulating people and circumstances to obtain my idea of what you want rather than submitting to your plan, which is always better than my own.*

Meditation passage for today: verse 29

Day 16—Genesis 28

After being sent away with the blessing of his father Isaac, Jacob went to his father's family in Haran, where he was to find his wife. It is ironic that this deceiver would be out-foxed by an even more consummate deceiver, his Uncle Laban.

On his way to Haran, Jacob encountered the presence of God in his dream about a ladder that reached to heaven. The Lord affirmed his covenant with Jacob, as he had done with Abraham and Isaac before him. The Lord promised to be with him and to preserve and protect him in all his undertakings, and Jacob realized that the place of his encounter with God was a special place, the house of God (Bethel).

READ GENESIS 28

Prayer: *Lord, how awesome is the "Son of Man upon whom the angels of God ascend and descend"! You keep your covenant and are personally involved in the affairs of your people. Let me walk with you and keep me in your way.*

Meditation passage for today: verses 12–16

Day 17—Genesis 37

It was painfully obvious that Joseph was his father Jacob's favorite son. When Joseph (perhaps unwisely) shared his dreams with his brothers, they hated him even more. It appeared that he had ambitions of ruling over them. When the brothers saw an opportunity to get rid of Joseph, their jealousy prompted them to sell him into slavery in Egypt, presumably never to be seen again. The conspirators lied to their father Jacob and claimed that Joseph had been killed by a wild beast. At first glance, it would appear that Joseph's dreams could never be fulfilled.

READ GENESIS 37

Prayer: *Lord, you orchestrate human circumstances according to a wisdom that transcends our understanding. May I learn to trust in your plans and purposes for my life, especially in times when the outcome seems doubtful.*

Meditation passage for today: verses 9–11

Day 18—Genesis 39

In spite of Joseph's trials, this account reveals that the Lord was with him and would not abandon him. Joseph found favor in Potiphar's sight, and the Egyptian's household prospered under Joseph's prudent management.

Potiphar's implicit trust in Joseph suddenly came to an end when his wife accused Joseph of attempted rape after Joseph refused her enticing offers. Joseph was rewarded with prison for his actual fidelity and moral character. Even there, the hand of the Lord remained upon him as he was being prepared for God's good purposes.

READ GENESIS 39

Prayer: *Lord, when I consider Joseph's difficulties, it is easy to see how he could have despaired and wondered if the dreams you gave him would ever be fulfilled. Give me the grace to cling to your character in times when my circumstances seem hopeless and pointless.*

Meditation passage for today: verses 2–3, 21

Day 19—Genesis 40

During his years of imprisonment, the Lord continued to nurture and prepare Joseph for a destiny far beyond anything he could imagine.

Joseph was not only a capable and prudent man, but he was also given the divine gift of being able to interpret dreams. When he correctly interpreted the dreams of Pharaoh's chief butler and chief baker, Joseph hoped that the butler would mention him to Pharaoh so that he would be extricated from the dungeon. Instead, he continued to languish in prison.

READ GENESIS 40

Prayer: *Lord, it is easy to read this account with complete hindsight and realize that everything you allowed in Joseph's life worked together for his ultimate good. Grant me the wisdom to see things more from your perspective and to view my temporal circumstances in light of your eternal purposes.*

Meditation passage for today: verse 8

Day 20—Genesis 41

Two years after the incident with the butler and baker, the Lord troubled Pharaoh with a disturbing dream that cried out for an interpretation. It was then that the butler recalled Joseph's ability to interpret dreams and informed Pharaoh about him.

When Pharaoh summoned Joseph, the Hebrew's fortunes changed suddenly and dramatically. Not only was he granted the ability to interpret Pharaoh's dreams, he was also given the wisdom to know how to act in the most effective way to avert the disastrous consequences of the coming famine in Egypt. In the course of only a few hours, Joseph was elevated from imprisonment to the position of prime minister in Egypt.

READ GENESIS 41

Prayer: *Lord, you are able to bring a person or a nation down in a day and to raise them up suddenly at your good pleasure. All things are in your hands, and I want to learn to take this to heart when I find myself discouraged and disheartened.*

Meditation passage for today: verses 16, 25, 28

Day 21—Genesis 42

The Lord used the great famine to orchestrate an encounter between Joseph and his brothers. When his brothers came and bowed down before him, Joseph remembered the dreams he had years before and realized they were being fulfilled.

Joseph tested his brothers to see what was in their hearts, and they did not realize who he was or that he could understand their language. He required them to leave Simeon in Egypt while they returned to Canaan to bring their youngest brother to confirm their words.

READ GENESIS 42

Prayer: *Lord, thank you for this very real account of the gradual process of reconciliation of estranged relationships. Help me to examine my own relationships and humble myself enough to seek out reconciliation and closure with anyone I have injured in the past.*

Meditation passage for today: verse 22

Day 22—Genesis 43

Jacob resisted sending his sons back to Egypt even though he knew that Simeon was detained there. He tried to avert action because he did not want to lose Benjamin, but the severity of the famine caused him to relent. Judah assured him that he would be responsible for Benjamin's welfare.

Once again Joseph's brothers prostrated themselves before him in fulfillment of the dreams he had been given. It was an emotional moment for Joseph to see his full brother Benjamin, and he sought to control himself during the serving of the meal.

READ GENESIS 43

Prayer: *Lord, I see how your purposeful hand intervenes in human affairs. Your plans are not thwarted by our disobedience and manipulation. Grant that I may rest in your care and entrust my affairs to you.*

Meditation passage for today: verse 14

Day 23—Genesis 44

Once again Joseph tested the hearts of his brothers to see how they would respond when he made a claim on Benjamin to be his slave. His brother Judah made good on his promise to Jacob to become surety for Benjamin, and when Joseph saw Judah's willingness to sacrifice himself to save Jacob from the grief of losing Benjamin, Joseph was ready to reveal himself to his brothers. Thus Joseph was able to witness the repentance and remorse of his brothers for the injury they had committed years earlier against him.

READ GENESIS 44

Prayer: *Lord, your servant Joseph dealt wisely with his brothers. This revealed that the hardship he had suffered had produced gradual character development. Help me to consider the long-term consequences of my actions, and teach me to treat others with mercy and grace.*

Meditation passage for today: verse 16

Day 24—Genesis 45

This chapter completes the process of reconciliation between Joseph and his brothers and reveals the power of forgiveness to restore estranged relationships. When Joseph revealed his true identity to his brothers, he also communicated the divine purpose of the pains he had experienced over the years: "Now do not be grieved or angry with yourselves because you sold me here, for God sent me before you to preserve life." Thus, Joseph was reunited with his brothers, and the children of Israel were brought into Egypt to prevent them from losing their identity through intermarriage with the Canaanites.

READ GENESIS 45

Prayer: *Lord, I marvel at the graciousness of your servant Joseph and at his willingness to extend forgiveness and grace to his brothers. Give me the wisdom to see things from your perspective, so I will not suppose that people injure me in ways that cannot be redeemed by your higher purposes.*

Meditation passage for today: verses 5, 7–8

Day 25—Genesis 50

At the end of Jacob's sojourn in Egypt, he blessed his sons in accordance with their character and the future of their tribes. Joseph made elaborate arrangements for Jacob's embalming and burial. A large retinue of Egyptian officials accompanied them for the solemn burial and lamentation in Canaan.

Sadly, Joseph's brothers assumed that their father Jacob was the restraining influence that kept Joseph from seeking vengeance on them for their sin against him. When they approached him after Jacob's death, Joseph had to assure them that although they meant evil against him, "God meant it for good in order to bring about this present result, to preserve many people alive."

READ GENESIS 50

Prayer: *Lord, thank you for Joseph's words of comfort, wisdom, and perspective to his brothers. Without your grace in my life, I am vulnerable to bitterness, resentment, and wrath when people intend evil against me.*

Meditation passage for today: verses 19–20

Day 26—Exodus 1

In the four centuries that transpired between Genesis 50 and Exodus 1, the condition of the children of Israel degenerated from one of privilege and protection to one of prejudice and bondage. The descendants of Jacob multiplied so rapidly that they became a threat to the Egyptians, who reacted by plotting to exterminate their male children. The oppression increased and the people of Israel lost all hope because of their forced labor and complete insecurity.

READ EXODUS 1

Prayer: *Lord, you often have to bring us to the end of ourselves before we will acknowledge our desperate condition and call upon you for deliverance. May I learn to respond quickly to you rather than resist you through my stubborn pride.*

Meditation passage for today: verses 8, 12

Day 27—Exodus 2

In this chapter, the focus shifts from the children of Israel as a whole to a specific family God would use to provide deliverance for his people. The Lord intervened in the life of the infant Moses, so that Pharaoh's daughter would raise this Hebrew child who was destined for death.

When Moses sought to deliver his people on his own timing and terms, he failed and had to flee for his life to the land of Midian. While he was there, his people back in Egypt remembered and cried out to the God of their fathers, to deliver them from bondage.

READ EXODUS 2

Prayer: *Lord, I see how you prepare to save your people even before they call upon your name. I thank you that you are concerned with the things that concern me, and that you always desire what is best for me.*

Meditation passage for today: verses 10, 23–25

Day 28—Exodus 3

After forty years of personal preparation in the wilderness of Midian, Moses was ready to become the leader and deliverer the Lord was grooming him to be. His personal encounter with the presence of the living God at the burning bush permanently transformed him and gave him a desire to seek the Lord for the remainder of his days. The great I AM commissioned Moses to represent the children of Israel before Pharaoh and to perform signs and wonders until Pharaoh would finally let the people go.

READ EXODUS 3

Prayer: *Lord, you are the God of Abraham, the God of Isaac, and the God of Jacob, the everlasting I AM WHO I AM. I thank you that you stoop to show compassion on your people and deliver them from their servitude to sin and death.*

Meditation passage for today: verses 6, 14–15

Day 29—Exodus 4

Moses repeatedly objected to becoming God's chosen instrument of deliverance for his people. The Lord answered each of his excuses. Moses' fifth objection to send someone else angered the Lord because of the lack of faith it represented. However, the Lord made provision for a spokesman to the people, and Aaron was already on his way to visit his brother Moses. When Moses and Aaron returned to Egypt, the Lord gave them favor with the children of Israel, who realized that the Lord had visited them and looked on their affliction.

READ EXODUS 4

Prayer: *Lord, you meet your people at their point of need and authenticate yourself in so many ways. Thank you that you prepare creative ways of delivering us from the servitude and monotony of sin, and that you invite us to participate in your works and ways.*

Meditation passage for today: verses 5, 11, 31

Day 30—Exodus 5

As the Lord had predicted, Pharaoh rejected Moses' request and denied the Lord, declaring, "Who is the Lord that I should obey his voice to let Israel go?" Matters turned even worse for the children of Israel when Pharaoh, accusing them of being lazy, mandated that the slaves must gather their own straw without reducing the daily quota of bricks. This naturally made Moses unpopular in his own people's sight; far from delivering them from their bondage, he had actually increased it. Not surprisingly, Moses complained to the Lord and wanted to resign his divine commission.

READ EXODUS 5

Prayer: *Lord, I know that when you show your people a new thing, you test them to see what is in their hearts. Teach me to look to you alone as my source of provision in all things and not to put my hope in people, possessions, or circumstances to deliver me.*

Meditation passage for today: verses 22–23

Day 31—Exodus 6

It often seems that the Lord does not work until we reach the end of our own resources. Now that all seemed lost, God assured Moses that he was about to guide his people out of Egypt with an outstretched arm and with great judgments. Hearing these words of assurance, Moses relayed them to his people, but in their anguish of spirit they would not heed him. Nevertheless, the Lord recommissioned Moses for the great task he was to undertake.

READ EXODUS 6

Prayer: *Lord, thank you that you revealed yourself to your people as Yahweh, the personal, covenant-keeping God who was, and is, and is to come, the Almighty. Thank you for your concern for our plight and our needs. May I always be responsive to your gracious initiative.*

Meditation passage for today: verses 2–8

Day 32—Exodus 7

After his negative experience with Pharaoh and his people, Moses needed reassurance from the Lord about his plan and purposes for his people. Moses was called into a significant leadership role, and he needed to lean solely on the Lord to accomplish this daunting task.

Pharaoh's magicians were able to accomplish just enough with their enchantments that Pharaoh could rationalize the miraculous signs of Aaron's rod and the first plague of blood as being religious chicanery. Just as the Lord had predicted, Pharaoh's heart grew hard.

READ EXODUS 7

Prayer: *Lord, you have complete authority over heaven and earth, and nothing is too difficult for you. When I review your mighty acts in history, it increases my confidence that you can work powerfully in my own life as well.*

Meditation passage for today: verses 4–5

Day 33—Exodus 8

The next three plagues—frogs, lice, and flies—added to Egypt's woes but failed to convince Pharaoh to release the children of Israel. The plague of lice induced the magicians themselves to recognize the finger of God, but Pharaoh's heart was hardened and he refused to heed them. Over and over the cycle repeated itself: the plague erupted, and Pharaoh tried to placate Moses with a measure of compromise so that order might be restored. But once the pests were gone, Pharaoh forgot all about his promises to Moses.

READ EXODUS 8

Prayer: *Lord, there appears to be no limit to the human propensity to deny and rationalize the truth, even when it is staring us in the face. May I not harden my heart and resist the things you wish to teach me. May I be sensitive and responsive to your desires.*

Meditation passage for today: verses 10, 19

Day 34—Exodus 9

As the plagues upon Egypt progressed, it became increasingly obvious that none of them affected the dwellings of the children of Israel in the land of Goshen. The mounting pressure upon Pharaoh was evident in his growing concessions to Moses, but he still refused to comply with Moses' full demands. After the pestilence on Egypt's livestock, the plague of boils, and finally the plague of severe hail, it appeared that Pharaoh would relent. However, Moses told him, "I know that you do not yet fear the Lord God."

READ EXODUS 9

Prayer: *Lord, the ability of people to resist and rebel against you is so great that it is frightening. Give me the wisdom to fear your Word and respond to the things you proclaim and exhort.*

Meditation passage for today: verses 12, 14

Day 35—Exodus 10

The pattern of the plagues shows a gradual increase in intensity and severity. With the growing devastation, Pharaoh's own servants urgently exhorted him to relent and accede to Moses' repeated request ("Do you not realize that Egypt is destroyed?"). But Pharaoh wanted to determine the terms of departure. The plague of locusts brought Pharaoh to the point of acknowledging his sin but not to the point of letting the Israelites go. The ninth plague carried a palpable darkness to the land followed by a final hardening of Pharaoh's heart.

READ EXODUS 10

Prayer: *Lord, no one is able to stand against you, though we often try to resist your purposes. Help me remember the fleeting and limited nature of human power and wealth in contrast to the permanent and infinite nature of your power and greatness.*

Meditation passage for today: verses 20, 27

Day 36—Exodus 11

In spite of nine awful plagues that decimated the land of Egypt, Pharaoh stubbornly refused to permit the people to depart. His pride brought on the devastation of his own nation.

It took the tenth plague—the death of the firstborn of every house in Egypt, including his own son—to cause the Pharaoh to relent. By this time, Moses had attained greatness in the sight of the Egyptians as well as his own people. Before they left Egypt, the people finally received their "wages" for their years of servitude by receiving articles of silver and gold from the Egyptians.

READ EXODUS 11

Prayer: *Lord, you accomplish your purposes in spite of our stubborn opposition. All life is in your hands; you give life and you take it away, and though we do not always understand your ways, we can always trust your good purposes.*

Meditation passage for today: verse 3

Day 37—Exodus 12

The images of Passover are a powerful portrait of redemption through sacrificial blood. The lamb had to be in its prime, without blemish, tested for a period of days, and sacrificed between 3:00 and 6:00 in the afternoon. The blood of the lamb had to be applied to the lintel and doorposts of each house so that the angel of death would spare the first-born.

The Passover lamb reminds us of the voluntary sacrifice of the Lamb of God, God's own Son, who takes away the sin of the world.

READ EXODUS 12

Prayer: *Lord, I thank you for this detailed prefiguring of the sacrificial death of your Son. On the night of the first Passover, you redeemed your people and set them free from their servitude. Through the blood of your Son, purify me as well, so that I would be free to serve you in love and truth.*

Meditation passage for today: verses 13–14, 26–27

Day 38—Exodus 13

The Feasts of Unleavened Bread and Passover marked the beginning of Israel as a redeemed nation before God. These feasts were instituted as an annual memorial of the Lord's mighty acts on his people's behalf. From then on, every firstborn animal would be set apart, and every firstborn son redeemed before the Lord.

When the Israelites set out, the Lord guided them through the wilderness to the Red Sea so they would not change their minds and return to Egypt. Had they gone the easier coastal way, the Egyptian army could easily have overwhelmed them.

READ EXODUS 13

Prayer: *Lord, you delight in deeds of deliverance and in providing life and hope for those who turn to you. May I walk in complete dependence upon you and not change my mind by seeking to return to the values and lusts of this world.*

Meditation passage for today: verses 9, 21–22

Day 39—Exodus 14

The children of Israel were horrified to discover that the army of Pharaoh was pursuing them through the wilderness. Once again, Pharaoh had changed his mind. When the people cried out in despair, Moses told them to stand still and see the salvation of the Lord.

The angel of God went behind them, and a pillar of cloud arose, a barrier of protection between the people of Israel and the Egyptian army. Throughout the night, the miracle of the parting of the Red Sea made it possible for the children of Israel to cross the sea on dry ground. The next morning the Lord closed the waters on the pursuing Egyptians and overthrew them. Thus, the Lord delivered his people through blood (the Passover) and through water (the Exodus).

READ EXODUS 14

Prayer: *Lord, you are the God of surprises. Just when it appears that all is lost, you do a new thing to deliver your people. May I learn to know not only your works but also your ways.*

Meditation passage for today: verses 13, 31

Day 40—Exodus 19

In the days that followed the Exodus, the Lord provided for his people and protected them in the wilderness. Now that they had been redeemed, they were to be set apart in a covenant relationship with God and instructed in his ways, so that they could become a holy people. God invited them to obey his voice and keep his covenant so that they would be a special treasure to him. The people were terrified when the Lord showed himself to them through thunder, lightning, a thick cloud, an earthquake, and the blast of a trumpet on Mount Sinai.

READ EXODUS 19

Prayer: *Lord, you are holy and awesome. The powers of nature point to your infinite power. When I draw near to you, I am in the presence of a consuming fire.*

Meditation passage for today: verses 5–6

Day 41—Exodus 20

The revelation of the Ten Commandments on Mount Sinai displayed the Lord's desire that his people reflect his perfection of character in their walk with him and with one another.

These commandments contain the essence of rightly ordered spiritual and social life. They are concerned not merely with external actions but also with internal attitudes. The first four commandments concern our relationship with God, and the last six commandments concern our relationships with the people in our lives. Human effort alone is not enough to observe all the commandments perfectly; we need the grace of God to fortify our resolve.

READ EXODUS 20

Prayer: *Lord, you are a community of three Persons whose perfect character is the absolute basis for the true, the beautiful, and the good. By your grace, may I invite you to display your character and righteousness through me.*

Meditation passage for today: verses 3, 5–6

Day 42—Exodus 32

After the Lord revealed his judgments and ratified his blood covenant with the people, Moses went up the mountain where he received the instructions for the tabernacle and the two tablets of the testimony.

During his forty–day absence, the people corrupted themselves and degenerated into idolatry. Moses interceded with the Lord on their behalf and disciplined them. In his love for the Lord, Moses appealed to the people to preserve God's reputation in the sight of the nations; in his love for his people, Moses cried out to the Lord to forgive them.

READ EXODUS 32

Prayer: *Lord, I confess I am prone to turn aside from walking with you, particularly when I am distracted by the cares of this world. Let my love for you cause me to be concerned with the honor of your name and to give you highest priority in the affairs of this life.*

Meditation passage for today: verses 12–13

Day 43—Leviticus 16

The Book of Leviticus was revealed at the foot of Mount Sinai as the Lord instructed his people in the ways of holiness. The moral, civil, and ceremonial laws were designed to provide order, stability, justice, and righteousness in the theocratic covenant community of Israel. These laws set them apart from all other nations.

Those who have been redeemed must also be sanctified, and the central provision for sanctification in Israel was the sacrificial system with the priesthood and the tabernacle. The holiest day of the year was Yom Kippur, the Day of Atonement, during which the consecrated high priest would enter the Holy Place with the blood of a goat as a sin offering for the people.

READ LEVITICUS 16

Prayer: *Lord, no one can approach your holiness without a clean heart, which is possible only because of the shed blood of your righteous Son, Jesus Christ. Thank you that I can boldly come to your throne of grace.*

Meditation passage for today: verses 16, 30

Day 44—Numbers 13

By this time, the Israelites were grumbling and complaining about their conditions, their food, and their leadership. The longer they were away, the more they idealized Egypt and wanted to return.

Numbers 13–14 marks a permanent change in the chosen people's destiny. While camped at Kadesh, the Israelites sent representatives from each of the twelve tribes to investigate the Promised Land. When the spies returned, the people were disheartened by the majority report. In spite of encouraging Caleb's words, the majority opinion prevailed and the people drew back in disbelief.

READ NUMBERS 13

Prayer: *Lord, I realize that the perspective I bring to my circumstances can make a big difference in the outcome. Grant that I may see things from a biblical point of view rather than a worldly perspective, so that I will trust you enough to obey you.*

Meditation passage for today: verse 30

Day 45—Numbers 14

Convinced that the Lord did not have their best interests at heart, the people wanted to select a leader who would guide them back to Egypt. Joshua and Caleb urged the congregation not to rebel against the Lord but to trust in his enough to protection as they obediently claimed the Promised Land.

Once again, Moses had to intercede for his people before the Lord, and once again the Lord pardoned the children of Israel. Nevertheless, there were grave consequences for their failure to believe God, and the generation of the Exodus lost its opportunity to be the generation of the conquest. From that point, everyone twenty years old and above would perish in the wilderness, and it would be their children who would conquer the land.

READ NUMBERS 14

Prayer: *Lord, it is frightening to realize that I can commit the sin of unused potential by drawing back in disbelief. I ask for the faith to honor you in spite of appearances to the contrary, and to believe that you always desire what is best for me.*

Meditation passage for today: verses 7–9, 18

Day 46—Deuteronomy 1

After an additional thirty–eight years of wandering in the wilderness, the new generation of Israelites needed to be prepared spiritually, morally, and physically to conquer the Promised Land. Near the end of his life, Moses taught the people in the plains of Moab and communicated God's ordinances, statutes, and testimonies a second time. Moses began his series of exhortations by reviewing God's dealings with his people since their time at Mount Sinai after the Exodus. He focused on the tragedy of disbelief at Kadesh and the consequences that followed.

READ DEUTERONOMY 1

Prayer: *Lord, I thank you that you instruct me in the way of life through your revealed Word. May I treasure your teachings and take them to heart so that my way will not be impeded by the sins of disbelief, autonomy, and rebellion.*

Meditation passage for today: verses 21, 29–31

Day 47—Deuteronomy 2

Moses continued his review of God's dealings among his people by reminding them of their encounters with the people of Edom, Moab, and Ammon. He reminded them of their conquest of Sihon and the Amorites to provide them with a sense of perspective on the way God had gone before them, guided them, provided for them, and protected them. The clearer they grasped God's faithfulness in the past, the better they would be able to trust him for the challenges of the present.

READ DEUTERONOMY 2

Prayer: *Lord, teach me to review your dealings with me in the past so that I will have enough perspective to trust you actively in the present. Give me a sanctified memory and a growing sense of gratitude for what you have done in my life.*

Meditation passage for today: verse 7

Day 48—Deuteronomy 3

After their conquest of Sihon, the Lord gave his people victory over Og and the people of Bashan. The tribes of Reuben and Gad as well as half the tribe of Manasseh possessed the land and cities that were conquered in the Transjordan. After these victories, Moses asked God to allow him to cross over and see the land beyond the Jordan before his death.

The Lord refused to do this because of Moses' disobedience when he struck the rock in anger at the grumbling of the people. Instead, the Lord allowed Moses to see the land from a distance at the top of Mount Pisgah across from Jericho.

READ DEUTERONOMY 3

Prayer: *Lord, your faithfulness, loyalty, and love for your people are great, in spite of the fact that we rarely appreciate what you have done for us. Teach me to treasure your mighty deeds and acts of lovingkindness in my heart.*

Meditation passage for today: verses 22, 24

Day 49—Deuteronomy 4

Moses exhorted the new generation in the plains of Moab to remember the things they had seen and to teach those things to their children and grandchildren. He also warned them against the insidious lure of idolatry and the human tendency to worship images of our own making rather than serve the invisible God. Sadly, Moses predicted that they would indeed succumb to idolatry and suffer the consequences: They would be scattered among the nations until they turned back to the Lord in their distress.

READ DEUTERONOMY 4

Prayer: *Lord, even in this day and age, the lure of idolatry beckons: money, power, and possessions, anything that draws my heart away from you. You are God in heaven above and on the earth below, and there is none other besides you. May I keep myself from every form of idolatry.*

Meditation passage for today: verses 6–9, 24, 35, 37, 39

Day 50—Deuteronomy 5

The Ten Commandments were previously revealed in Exodus 20, and Moses reviews them here for the sake of the new generation that is being prepared to conquer the Promised Land. These commandments were not designed to oppress the people but to give them the freedom of appropriate boundaries in their relationships with God and with each other.

God always wants what is best for his people: "Oh that they had such a heart in them, that they would fear me and keep all my commandments always, that it may be well with them and with their sons forever!" The Lord's desire is that his children would enjoy life by ordering their steps according to his good ways.

READ DEUTERONOMY 5

Prayer: *Lord, I know that you always want what is best for your people and that you desire us to cling firmly to you and not stray from the way that leads to life. Give me the power to walk in the Spirit and so fulfill your royal law.*

Meditation passage for today: verses 24, 29, 33

Day 51—Deuteronomy 6

God gave the children of Israel his commandments to protect the well-being and longevity of his people. He knew that if they loved him with all their hearts, it would spill over into their homes and into their habits. If they trusted him as the source of all their benefits, he would lead them into the Promised Land and bless them with every kind of abundance.

READ DEUTERONOMY 6

Prayer: *Lord, your commandments lead your people to do what is in our best interests. Help me remember that you are never the enemy of my joy and well-being, but rather that you are the source of all that is best for me.*

Meditation passage for today: verses 4–7, 23

Day 52—Deuteronomy 7

The Lord warned his people not to participate in the heathen practices of the nations that the Israelites had been sent to conquer. His people were not to intermarry with the nations but were to sustain their separate identity as a holy community, dedicated to God. They were to remain "a people for his own possession out of all the peoples on the face of the earth." The Lord reminded them that he did not love them for their size or virtue, but simply because he chose to do so. His desire was to bless them in all ways, as long as they remained faithful to him.

READ DEUTERONOMY 7

Prayer: *Lord, I am thankful that the love you bestowed on your people was not elicited by anything they had achieved or merited. Since your love is unearned, I cannot diminish or increase it, and therefore I am secure in your grace.*

Meditation passage for today: verses 6–9

Day 53—Deuteronomy 8

The theme of remembrance recurs often in the Old Testament, because God knows that embedded in human nature is a tendency to forget. Nothing ages more quickly than gratitude; given a little time, people have a way of reducing grace into entitlement. Therefore Moses exhorted the generation of the conquest to remember God's benefits. They were warned not to slip into the arrogance of supposing in their hearts, "My power and the strength of my hand made me this wealth." It is the Lord God who gave them the ability to create wealth; if they forgot this, he could easily take it away.

READ DEUTERONOMY 8

Prayer: *Lord, I ask for the grace to remember all of your benefits and to realize that everything I have comes from you. Prevent me from being tempted to slip into the delusion that I achieved these things without you.*

Meditation passage for today: verses 3, 18

Day 54—Deuteronomy 27

After reviewing the commandments, testimonies, and statutes with the new generation, Moses instructed them to write all the words of the Law on large whitewashed stones after they crossed the Jordan River. These stones would serve as an altar and a reminder about the covenant commitment they had entered into with the Lord their God. Six of the tribes were to proclaim blessings for obedience from Mount Gerizim, and six of the tribes were to proclaim cursings for disobedience from Mount Ebal. It was essential for their well-being that they obeyed the voice of the Lord and observed his commandments.

READ DEUTERONOMY 27

Prayer: *Lord, help me see that you are serious about the things you exhort your children to know, be, and do. Let me realize with greater clarity the blessings of obedience and the consequences of disobedience.*

Meditation passage for today: verse 10

Day 55—Deuteronomy 28

The list of blessings for obedience in the theocratic covenant community is impressive, extending to every realm of life: physical, economic, social, and political. However, the list of cursings for disobedience in the same community of faith is equally impressive and just as all-pervasive. It is clear that much will be required of those to whom much has been given. Sadly, Moses knew which way the people would eventually turn, and that the Lord would scatter the people of Israel among the nations because of their disobedience to his covenant.

READ DEUTERONOMY 28

Prayer: *Lord, let this list of blessings and cursings be a sober reminder to me that right now counts forever. The quality of my walk with you in this life will have an impact on the rewards I receive when I stand to give an account to your Son.*

Meditation passage for today: verses 1, 58

Day 56—Deuteronomy 29

Nearing the end of his lengthy discourse to the people, Moses reminds them that it is the Lord who established his covenant with them and that they entered into it willingly. The Lord's desire was to establish them as a people for himself, but Moses made it clear that they would eventually forsake the Lord their God and experience the devastating adversity consequent to serving other gods. This chapter is a reminder that "God is not mocked; for whatever a man sows, this he will also reap" (Gal 6:7).

READ DEUTERONOMY 29

Prayer: *Lord, I know that this life is not a dress rehearsal but is very real in its nature and consequences. By your grace, I want to make my time count for eternity by treasuring you and obeying the things you ask me to do.*

Meditation passage for today: verses 9, 13, 29

Day 57—Deuteronomy 30

Moses concludes his sermons to the people by predicting that the Lord would drive the Israelites into future captivity among the nations. Eventually they would be led to repentance and restoration from captivity.

Moses exhorts the Israelites to choose between life and death, good and evil, blessing and cursing, to love God or to abandon him; at the same time, he reminds them of the consequences of those choices. Moses urges his people to love and obey God so that they will dwell and prosper in the land.

READ DEUTERONOMY 30

Prayer: *Lord, you dealt with Israel by relating material benefits and loss to obedience and disobedience. I realize that in the body of Christ, the blessings for obedience relate more to the fruit of the Spirit than to the fruit of the vine. Let me walk by your Spirit and enjoy his benefits.*

Meditation passage for today: verses 11–16, 19–20

Day 58—Deuteronomy 32

The song of Moses was a sad and realistic indictment against the people that reminded them of their rich heritage and their repeated tendency to forget the God who fathered them. Their idolatry provoked the Lord to jealousy, since he wanted his people to be wholly his. "See now that I, I am he, and there is no god besides me; it is I who put to death and give life. I have wounded and it is I who heal, and there is no one who can deliver from my hand." Obedience to God's words was their very life, but disobedience and rebellion would lead to death.

READ DEUTERONOMY 32

Prayer: *Lord, my life is hidden with you in the heavenly places in Christ. May I look to Christ, abide in him, and draw my sustenance from him in all things.*

Meditation passage for today: verses 4, 39

Day 59—Deuteronomy 34

Moses blessed the children of Israel before going up to Mount Nebo to die. After reminding them of the Lord's great love for them, this humble servant of the Lord was granted a miraculous vision of the entire Promised Land even as far as the Mediterranean Sea. The Lord himself buried Moses in an unmarked place. Before his death, Moses laid his hands on his protégé, Joshua, who had been endued with the spirit of wisdom. Moses enjoyed a unique relationship with the Lord, in that the Lord knew him face-to-face.

READ DEUTERONOMY 34

Prayer: *Lord, I am grateful for your dedicated and obedient servant Moses. You continue to use us, in spite of our lapses, when we return to you. Thank you for your grace, which gives me fidelity to you and your purposes.*

Meditation passage for today: verses 10–12

Day 60—Joshua 1

As soon as Joshua assumed the mantle of Moses, he faced the daunting task of leading the children of Israel across the Jordan River to begin their conquest of the Promised Land. The Lord himself encouraged Joshua and exhorted him to be strong and of good courage. The key to Joshua's success rested in his relationship with the Lord, and therefore he needed to be a man of the Word who meditated on it day and night. By cultivating his daily walk with God, Joshua would be a fit leader to guide the people into the inheritance the Lord had promised to them.

READ JOSHUA 1

Prayer: *Lord, thank you for the wealth of your Word. Like Joshua, I want to be shaped by your Word. I want to keep it before me so that I will "observe to do according to all that is written in it."*

Meditation passage for today: verses 7–9

Day 61—Joshua 2

The story of Rahab the harlot is a remarkable account of a woman who applied the little she knew about the God of Israel. Rahab took the risk of protecting the two Israelite spies who came to investigate the city of Jericho. When she hid them on the roof of her house on the city wall, Rahab acknowledged that "the Lord your God, he is God in heaven above and on earth beneath." She asked for the reward of protection when Israel overtook her city, and they instructed her to bind a line of scarlet cord in her window as a token against that day. She and her household were spared (see Joshua 6), and she is mentioned in Matthew 1 as being a part of the messianic line, and in Hebrews 11 and James 2 as an example of faith in action.

READ JOSHUA 2

Prayer: *Lord, I thank you for the example of simple faith of this Gentile woman who put her complete trust in you. Thank you for honoring those who honor you.*

Meditation passage for today: verse 11

Day 62—Joshua 3

Joshua demonstrated his leadership and confidence in the Lord in this account of the crossing of the Jordan River. The Lord established Joshua's authority in the eyes of the children of Israel when Joshua obediently followed his instructions about commanding the priests to bear the ark of the covenant to the edge of the water. When the soles of the feet of the priests touched the overflowing waters of the river, the Lord cut off the flow of water until all the people were able to cross the riverbed on dry ground. Just as Moses led the people safely through the waters of the Red Sea, so his successor Joshua led them safely through the waters of the Jordan River.

READ JOSHUA 3

Prayer: *Lord, you are the supremely worthy object of trust, since you have demonstrated the truth of your promises again and again in the Bible's history of redemption. Let me remember your wonderful works among the sons of men.*

Meditation passage for today: verse 10

Day 63—Joshua 4

The Lord instructed Joshua to commemorate the Israelites' miraculous crossing of the Jordan River. Joshua did this by appointing representatives from each of the twelve tribes to carry a stone from the middle of the Jordan riverbed to Gilgal beyond the western shore. The pile of rocks would be a sign of God's faithfulness for the coming generations.

In addition, Joshua had the people set up twelve stones in the midst of the Jordan before the waters returned. When the priests came up from the riverbed, the waters of the Jordan returned and once again overflowed the banks. Thus, Joshua's authority was permanently established among the people.

READ JOSHUA 4

Prayer: *Lord, thank you that you have shown us your mighty hand, that we should fear you forever. You have accomplished great things for your people, and all your ways are righteous and true.*

Meditation passage for today: verses 14, 24

Day 64—Joshua 6

After Joshua had an encounter with the commander of the army of the Lord at the end of Joshua 5, he received the Lord's instructions as to how to conquer the walled city of Jericho. Everything about this conquest was unorthodox. It is significant that while the later battles under Joshua demonstrate great military tactics, this first battle had to be won solely by faith and obedience to the Lord. Thus, it would be clear from the outset that all the battles of Joshua had to be fought in the Lord's strength and not in dependence on human skill and abilities. God honored Israel's obedience to his apparently strange instructions, and this was one of the great moments in Israel's history.

READ JOSHUA 6

Prayer: *Lord, this account teaches me about the whole nature of living the spiritual life. Forgive me for depending upon my own skill and abilities. Teach me always to walk in childlike trust and obedience, looking to you for the victory.*

Meditation passage for today: verse 27

Day 65—Joshua 23

Nearing the end of his life, Joshua called the elders and leaders of Israel to give them a final message of exhortation and encouragement to remain faithful to the ways of the Lord. He reminded them that it is the Lord who fought for them, and that their relationship to him will be determinative of their continued success in the land. They needed the courage to keep and to do all that was written in the Book of the Law of Moses and to love the Lord. Otherwise they would descend into the morass of idolatry and intermarry with the remnant of the nations they were called to conquer. Just as the Lord had been faithful to them, so they had to be faithful to him.

READ JOSHUA 23

Prayer: *Lord, teach me fidelity to the spiritual disciplines of prayer and of time in your Word. Without these disciplines I will be vulnerable to the lures of this world system and tempted to turn away from you as my first love. May I hold fast to you and love you above all things.*

Meditation passage for today: verses 6, 14

Day 66—Joshua 24

Many begin well and end poorly, but Joshua finished his race well and remained faithful to the Lord throughout his 110 years.

In his message to the leaders of his people, Joshua reminded them of the Lord's gracious and powerful works on behalf of the children of Israel. With this perspective fresh in their minds, Joshua then exhorted his countrymen to fear the Lord, to serve him in sincerity and truth, and to put away all forms of idolatry. Joshua warned the people that the Lord is a jealous God who will not endure faithlessness or rebellion. The Israelites vowed to serve the Lord, and Joshua made a covenant with them.

READ JOSHUA 24

Prayer: *Lord, it is clear that the only options before me are service to you or service to idolatry. Help me not to put anything in the created order higher in my affections and priorities than you. Help me remember that you are a jealous God who will not let your children stray from you without disciplining them.*

Meditation passage for today: verses 14–15

Day 67—Judges 2

During the days of the judges, "there was no king in Israel; everyone did what was right in his own eyes." This book records the results of the Israelites' turning away from the Lord through apostasy, idolatry, and immorality.

After the death of Joshua and the elders of his generation, the children of Israel succumbed to the lure of idolatry and served the gods of the surrounding nations. They went through several cycles that moved from sin (idolatry), to servitude (oppression by a foreign power), to supplication (the people would finally cry to the Lord), to salvation (the Lord would raise up a deliverer–judge), to silence (a period of rest), until the cycle began once again after the death of the judge.

READ JUDGES 2

Prayer: *Lord, the cycles in the Book of Judges illustrate the monotony of sin and the creativity of your saving works on behalf of your people. May I not linger under sin's dominion, but quickly return to you when I fall into disobedience.*

Meditation passage for today: verse 7

Day 68–Judges 6

When the Lord raised up the Midianites to oppress the people of Israel due to their unfaithfulness to him, they finally cried out to God after seven years. In response, the Lord sent a prophet who rebuked them for their infidelity and also sent the angel of the Lord to commission Gideon.

Gideon became Israel's deliverer from the power of the Midianites. He followed the Lord's instructions to tear down the altar of Baal and to build an altar to the Lord. Gideon sent messengers to gather an army to defeat the Midianites and requested two evidences to assure himself that he was indeed being called by the Lord.

READ JUDGES 6

Prayer: *Lord, twice you condescended to respond to Gideon's request for a sign. Thank you that you do not wait until our faith is perfect before you call us. Thank you for revealing yourself to those who truly want to know you.*

Meditation passage for today: verses 22–23

Day 69—Judges 7

Knowing the human tendency to depend upon our own resources rather than trust in the Lord, God instructed Gideon to reduce the size of his army by allowing those who were fearful to return home. Even so, the ten thousand who remained were still too numerous, so the Lord reduced their number to three hundred. It was against these impossible odds that the Lord decided to act.

Once again, God gave Gideon a sign to encourage him. When the three hundred blew their trumpets and broke their pitchers, holding torches in their left hands and trumpets in their right hands, the Lord completely routed the Midianite armies. Thus it was the sword of the Lord that defeated their enemies.

READ JUDGES 7

Prayer: *Lord, this passage teaches that it is not possible for us to wage spiritual warfare effectively in the power of the flesh. Help me remember to stand firm in Christ, to submit to you, and to resist the world, the flesh, and the devil in your strength.*

Meditation passage for today: verse 2

Day 70—Judges 14

The visit of the angel of the Lord to Manoah and his wife, as recorded in Judges 13, made clear that Samson was set apart for the Lord before he was conceived. It was through this remarkable figure that the Lord began to deliver Israel out of the hand of the Philistines. Samson's penchant for foreign women provided an occasion to move against the Philistines. In this chapter, the Spirit of the Lord came mightily upon Samson when he was attacked by a lion and when he went down to Ashkelon to kill thirty of the Philistines.

READ JUDGES 14

Prayer: *Lord, you accomplish your purposes in spite of human shortcomings. May I be reminded that any good we accomplish is due to your Spirit at work in us.*

Meditation passage for today: verse 4

Day 71—Judges 15

In his anger in losing his Philistine wife, Samson wreaked havoc by releasing three hundred foxes with torches tied between their tails in the grain fields, vineyards, and olive groves of the Philistines. When they responded by burning Samson's former wife and father–in–law, Samson slaughtered many of the Philistines. Samson allowed his fearful Israelite countrymen to tie him with new ropes and deliver him into the hands of the Philistines. The Spirit of the Lord came mightily upon him, and he killed a thousand of them with the jawbone of a donkey.

READ JUDGES 15

Prayer: *Lord, you fulfill your plans through varied and unexpected means. The strangeness of this account reminds me that your ways among the sons of men are surprising and unpredictable.*

Meditation passage for today: verses 14, 19

Day 72—Judges 16

Once again, Samson had a liaison with a Philistine woman, and again the Lord delivered him from a death trap. The story of his uprooting and carrying the huge city gate of Gaza over thirty miles to Hebron is understated.

Samson's final relationship with a Philistine woman led to his downfall. Delilah was a persuasive and persistent woman who would not cease to manipulate him. Eventually she discovered the source of his strength and was able to sell him into the hands of the Philistine lords. Each time, Samson came closer to the truth, until he made the fatal mistake of revealing his secret and presuming that God would once again deliver him. Nevertheless, Samson was allowed to have a final victory against three thousand of his enemies.

READ JUDGES 16

Prayer: *Lord, this tragic story makes me wonder about the potential of this man had he walked in obedience to your ways. I realize you use us in spite of ourselves and not because of our abilities. Let me remember to walk in your strength and not in my own.*

Meditation passage for today: verses 28, 30

Day 73—Ruth 1

The story of Ruth and Boaz is a beautiful cameo of character, courage, and commitment during the days of the judges. It is a gem whose brilliance is enhanced by contrast to the darkness of the backdrop when "everyone did what was right in his own eyes."

Because of a famine in Bethlehem (which in Hebrew means "house of bread"), Elimelech took his wife Naomi and their two sons across the Jordan River to the country of Moab. After losing her husband and sons, Naomi decided to return to Bethlehem since the famine had broken. Ruth, one of her Moabite daughters-in-law, refused to remain in Moab, but risked everything out of love for Naomi, and followed her to Bethlehem.

READ RUTH 1

Prayer: *Lord, I thank you for the love of Ruth for Naomi and for her willingness to say, "Your people shall be my people, and your God, my God." May I too abandon myself to you and your loving purposes.*

Meditation passage for today: verses 16–17

Day 74—Ruth 2

The sovereign and purposeful hand of God is behind each of the scenes in the Book of Ruth. When Ruth sought to glean in the fields after the reapers, she "happened" to come to the portion of the field belonging to Naomi's kinsman Boaz. Impressed by what he had heard about Ruth's commitment to her mother–in–law, Boaz promised to protect her. In addition, Boaz provided for her through his instructions to his men. It was obvious to Naomi when Ruth returned from the field that someone had taken notice of her. When she heard it was her kinsman Boaz, the formerly embittered Naomi blessed the Lord for his kindness.

READ RUTH 2

Prayer: *Lord, this story reminds me that you are at work in ways I cannot predict or imagine. When I am tempted to be embittered at my circumstances, let me remember that you are working all things together for my good and that the only safe refuge is under your wings.*

Meditation passage for today: verses 12, 20

Day 75—Ruth 3

Naomi was a shrewd woman who analyzed the situation and knew what had to be done. She instructed her daughter-in-law to dress up and wait until Boaz had finished eating and drinking in celebration of the barley harvest. Then she was to cast herself on his mercy under cover of darkness and await his response. Ruth obediently followed Naomi's instructions, and when Boaz discovered her at his feet at midnight, he blessed her for not going after younger men. He would act as her *goel*, her kinsman-redeemer, if her nearer kinsman would not perform this duty for her. Before sending her back to Naomi, Boaz gave Ruth a generous supply of barley.

READ RUTH 3

Prayer: *Lord, let Boaz remind us of your creative and redemptive work on behalf of the people upon whom you have set your love. Like Ruth, let me be obedient to the role you call me to play.*

Meditation passage for today: verses 10–11

Day 76—Ruth 4

As Naomi predicted, Boaz would not rest until he had both redeemed the land Naomi had sold and married Ruth. Since there was a nearer kinsman, Boaz first had to offer the right of redemption to him. This must have been a tense moment for him, since he had come to love Ruth. At first the nearer kinsman agreed to redeem the land, but then declined when he found he would also have to raise an inheritance through Ruth. Boaz then formalized his commitment to act as Ruth's kinsman–redeemer before the elders at the city gate, and they blessed him. Significantly, Obed, the son of Ruth and Boaz, would become the grandfather of King David.

READ RUTH 4

Prayer: *Lord, I thank you that this story which began in tragedy and apparent hopelessness ended in joy and hope. In your grace, you took this Gentile woman and made her a direct part of the messianic line. You accomplish far more than what we ask or think.*

Meditation passage for today: verses 11–12, 14

Day 77—1 Samuel 1

Hannah's grief in being barren was amplified by the taunts she received year after year from her rival Peninnah, the other wife of Elkanah. It was particularly painful when she had to go up to the house of the Lord in Jerusalem each year with the rest of the family. In her bitterness of soul, she prayed to the Lord and made a vow that if the Lord granted her the gift of a son, she would dedicate him to the Lord's service. When Eli the priest realized her anguish, he blessed her and said, "May the God of Israel grant your petition that you have asked of him." The Lord fulfilled her request, and Hannah fulfilled her vow by presenting the child for the Lord's service after she had weaned him.

READ 1 SAMUEL 1

Prayer: *Lord, I thank you that you care for us and are concerned with the things that concern us. May I be anxious for nothing, but in everything by prayer and supplication, with thanksgiving, I will make my requests known to you.*

Meditation passage for today: verses 10, 17

Day 78—1 Samuel 2

Hannah's prayer of thanksgiving, similar to the *Magnificat* of Mary in Luke 1, is one of the great prayers of the Bible. She extolled the name and character of the Lord and acknowledged his sovereignty over all things. The Lord later granted her the gift of sons and daughters because of her faithfulness.

By contrast, the sons of Eli were unfaithful priests whose wickedness desecrated the sanctuary of the Lord. The Lord sent a man of God to rebuke Eli for his failure to discipline his sons. Since he dishonored the Lord in this way, the Lord would judge him and his sons.

READ 1 SAMUEL 2

Prayer: *Lord, your Word reveals the entire range of human character traits from fidelity and integrity to rebellion and treachery. Let me remember that you honor those who honor you, and that those who despise you will be lightly esteemed.*

Meditation passage for today: verses 2, 6–7, 30

Day 79—1 Samuel 3

Now the boy Samuel was growing in stature and in favor both with the Lord and with men" (1 Sm 2:26; see Lk 2:52). As a lad, Samuel ministered to the Lord before Eli, and on one significant night, he heard the voice of the Lord. Thinking Eli had called him, he ran to Eli who sent him back. After this happened three times, Eli realized that the voice was that of the Lord and told Samuel to say, "Speak, Lord, for your servant is listening." The Lord gave Samuel a message of judgment for Eli, and Samuel reluctantly relayed this prophetic message of condemnation.

READ 1 SAMUEL 3

Prayer: *Lord, I acknowledge your holiness and my need to treat you as holy. Keep me from besmirching your name in the sight of others by allowing sin to reign in my life.*

Meditation passage for today: verse 19

Day 80—1 Samuel 8

It is ironic that when Samuel grew old, his two sons became as treacherous and rebellious as Eli's two sons had been when Samuel was a boy. The people of Israel did not want Samuel's sons to succeed him as judges but instead clamored for a king to rule over them like all the nations. Thus, Israel rejected the theocracy and opted for a monarchy. Samuel warned them of the consequences of this action and what it would cost them to submit to the authority of an earthly king. The people refused to listen to Samuel's warning and insisted on having a visible king to judge them and fight their battles. The Lord instructed Samuel to listen to them and grant their request.

READ 1 SAMUEL 8

Prayer: *Lord, I realize that it is easy to clamor for things you know are not best for me. By your grace, protect me from myself so that I will not pursue something I will later live to regret.*

Meditation passage for today: verses 7–8

Day 81—1 Samuel 9

The Lord had already selected the man whom Samuel would anoint as Israel's first king. Saul was a handsome, tall, and imposing figure who had all the appearance and potential of an impressive ruler. God used the incident of Kish's lost donkeys as a means of drawing Saul to seek out Samuel the seer. Before Saul arrived, the Lord told Samuel that he was sending him the man he was to anoint as ruler over the people. Samuel sat Saul in the place of honor at the feast and later talked with him to prepare him to hear the word of God for him.

READ 1 SAMUEL 9

Prayer: *Lord, help me to pay close attention to my circumstances and seek you for direction. Let me be sensitive and responsive to your guidance so that I will not miss what you have for me.*

Meditation passage for today: verse 16

Day 82—1 Samuel 10

S amuel took Saul aside and privately anointed him with a flask of oil to be the ruler over the Lord's inheritance. Samuel predicted the immediate course of events and instructed Saul as to what to do. A transforming moment would take place when the Spirit of the Lord would come upon him and turn him into another man. After the Spirit of God came upon Saul and he prophesied among the prophets, Samuel called the people together to behold the man God had set apart to become their king. When they saw his impressive appearance, they shouted and said, "Long live the king!"

READ 1 SAMUEL 10

Prayer: *Lord, keep me from looking at people and circumstances from an outward and superficial perspective. I ask that the mind of Christ would grow in me, and that I would come to see things more from a biblical perspective.*

Meditation passage for today: verses 6, 19

Day 83—1 Samuel 15

K ing Saul began well, but it did not take him long to slip into the sin of disobedience by buckling under outward pressure (see 1 Sm 13). Samuel later gave Saul specific instructions to utterly destroy Amalek and all that he had, but Saul made the presumptuous decision to redefine the Lord's commands by sparing Agag and saving the best of the spoil. This act of rebellion marked the turning point in Saul's life, and the hand of the Lord was no longer upon him. In spite of Saul's excuses and sorrow, the kingdom would be torn from him and given to a better man who would obey the Lord.

READ 1 SAMUEL 15

Prayer: *Lord, help me see the danger in rationalizing disobedience by redefining your commands. Please keep me from the sins of presumption and rebellion so that I will walk in the obedience of humility.*

Meditation passage for today: verses 22–23, 29

Day 84—1 Samuel 16

Now that Saul had disqualified himself as God's anointed ruler over the people of Israel, the Lord instructed Samuel to go and anoint the man who would replace him as king. When Samuel was sent to Bethlehem to determine which of Jesse's sons God had selected to replace Saul as king, he looked at Eliab and assumed that he must be the Lord's anointed. Then God told Samuel, "Do not look at his appearance or at the height of his stature, because I have rejected him; for God sees not as man sees, for man looks at the outward appearance, but the Lord looks at the heart." It was David, Jesse's youngest son, who was destined for the throne, and David soon began to serve Saul.

READ 1 SAMUEL 16

Prayer: *Lord, without you it is impossible for me to see things as they truly are. Since I can only judge on the basis of outward appearance, I ask that you would guide my decisions and direction.*

Meditation passage for today: verse 7

Day 85—1 Samuel 17

The Philistine threat loomed large when they put forward a giant of a champion to discourage and taunt the armies of Israel. Goliath's defiant challenge brought great fear to the Israelite camp, and no one was willing to rise to fight the giant. When David heard about this, he was dismayed that this Philistine was successfully defying the armies of the living God. David's complete trust in the Lord gave him a confidence and perspective that the rest of his countrymen lacked. He told Goliath that the Lord would deliver him into his hand, and his defeat of Goliath encouraged the men of Israel and Judah to pursue the Philistines to their own territory.

READ 1 SAMUEL 17

Prayer: *Lord, this thrilling story reminds me once again that it is not the size of my opposition that matters but the power of my God. Let me walk in dependence upon the power of your Spirit and put my confidence entirely in you.*

Meditation passage for today: verses 26, 36, 46

Day 86—2 Samuel 5

After the death of King Saul, David was publicly anointed king over the tribes of Judah and Benjamin. However, the ten northern tribes of Israel continued for seven years and six months to support the house of Saul, while the house of David continued to grow in strength.

With the death of Saul's son Ishbosheth, the ten tribes of Israel gathered at Hebron and anointed David king over all Israel. David defeated the Jebusites and made Jerusalem his capital city. He then decisively defeated Israel's long–standing Philistine enemies by inquiring of the Lord and obediently carrying out God's instructions.

READ 2 SAMUEL 5

Prayer: *Lord, David illustrates that patient obedience and dependence on you is the pathway of life. May I wait upon you, depend upon your timing and strength, and obey all that you tell me to do.*

Meditation passage for today: verses 2, 12

Day 87—2 Samuel 7

After David had firmly established his kingdom and attained rest from his enemies, his thoughts turned to honoring the Lord by building a permanent temple in Jerusalem. This temple was to replace the tabernacle that had been built in the days of Moses. However, the Lord told David through Nathan the prophet that it would not be he but his son after him who would build a house for his name. Instead of David building a house for God, it was God who would establish a house and a kingdom for David and for his descendants after him. David responded to this covenant God was making with him and his seed by praising the greatness of the Lord God and asking for God's name to be magnified forever.

READ 2 SAMUEL 7

Prayer: *Lord, I thank you for this Davidic covenant, because it is perfectly fulfilled in the Person and work of the Lord Jesus. Indeed, in Jesus, the Root and the offspring of David, you have established the throne of David's kingdom forever.*

Meditation passage for today: verses 12–16, 22

Day 88—2 Samuel 11

David's victories over his enemies made him vulnerable to the troubling question, "Where do I go from here?" The middle-aged king decided not to lead his men in battle against the Ammonites but to remain at the palace in Jerusalem while Joab led his men instead. In his weakened spiritual condition, he succumbed not only to the sin of adultery but also to the sin of murder so that he could claim Bathsheba for himself. By disposing of Uriah the Hittite, one of his thirty mighty men, David supposed that his sin would not be discovered.

READ 2 SAMUEL 11

Prayer: *Lord, your Word shows that the flesh is neither improved nor removed in this life, and that the one who thinks he stands should take heed lest he fall. By your grace, let me cultivate a passion for Jesus so that I will not slip into despondency and succumb to temptation.*

Meditation passage for today: verse 11

Day 89–2 Samuel 12

Months passed and Bathsheba bore David a son. By this time, the king must have supposed that he had evaded the potential consequences of his sins against God, and against Bathsheba and her husband Uriah. But the Lord sent Nathan the prophet, who related a parable that incited the king and exposed the extent of his hidden guilt.

When he realized that the parable was actually about him, David repented (see Ps 51) and acknowledged his sin against the Lord. Nathan told him that the consequences for his sin would be the loss of the child born out of adultery as well as division in his own household. The Lord in his grace comforted Bathsheba with another son—the great Solomon, who would carry on the Davidic dynasty.

READ 2 SAMUEL 12

Prayer: *Lord, in your grace and mercy, you are quick to forgive. I pray that I will not presume on your grace, supposing that I can get away with the consequences of folly. I know that you discipline those whom you love so that we will be partakers of your holiness.*

Meditation passage for today: verses 13–14, 23

Day 90—1 Kings 1

As David was declining, his kingdom was in jeopardy of usurpation by Adonijah. David had made it clear that Solomon was to be his successor (see 1 Chr 22), and Nathan the prophet was alarmed about this course of events that was taking place without David's knowledge. He quickly acted by arranging for Bathsheba to speak to David on behalf of Solomon and then appearing before the king himself. The king responded by arranging for Zadok the priest and Nathan the prophet to anoint Solomon king and to have him sit on David's throne before the people. When Adonijah saw that his plot to take the throne was defeated, he requested and received mercy from the new King Solomon.

READ 1 KINGS 1

Prayer: *Lord, in spite of all multiplied human efforts to act independently of you and to refuse to heed your Word, your sovereign purposes are never thwarted by the devices and desires of men. I thank you that your Word is truth, and that nothing can prevent it from being fulfilled.*

Meditation passage for today: verses 29–30, 48

Day 91—1 Kings 2

Just before his death, David exhorted Solomon to remain faithful and obedient to the Lord. He also instructed his son to deal with those who had troubled him. Adonijah, Solomon's older half–brother who had plotted to claim the throne, made a foolish request through Bathsheba that led to his execution. Solomon also removed Abiathar from the priesthood for his infidelity to David, and he executed Joab for defecting to Adonijah and for his earlier wickedness in murdering Abner and Amasa. Finally, Solomon restricted Shimei, who had publicly cursed David, and executed him when he violated the restriction. Thus, King Solomon firmly established his throne.

READ 1 KINGS 2

Prayer: *Lord, these men reaped what they had sown and received justice for their acts of treachery. I ask you to treat me with mercy and not justice and to preserve me in the grace of your pardon.*

Meditation passage for today: verse 3

Day 92—1 Kings 3

When the Lord appeared to Solomon in a dream, he offered to grant Solomon one request. Solomon, aware of his own lack of experience and the burden of leadership that had been thrust upon him, requested an understanding heart to judge God's people with discernment. The Lord was pleased with this request for wisdom and told Solomon that he not only would be granted unprecedented wisdom, he would also receive what he had not asked. This great gift of wisdom was soon demonstrated publicly in Solomon's prudent judgment in the case of the two women who claimed the same child.

READ 1 KINGS 3

Prayer: *Lord, Solomon's humble request illustrates the truth that when we seek first your kingdom and your righteousness, the other needs of this life will be provided. Let me desire above all else the one thing most needful—the wisdom of trust in you.*

Meditation passage for today: verses 9, 14

Day 93—1 Kings 8

King David had collected the materials necessary for the building of the temple, and it took Solomon seven years to construct and furnish it. The temple was a costly achievement of great beauty, a structure that must have been magnificent to behold. When Solomon gathered the elders of Israel to watch the priests bring the ark of the covenant into the Most Holy Place, the awesome glory of God filled the temple. Solomon then offered a sermon and a great prayer of dedication, in which he entreated the Lord to hear the supplications of his people and to forgive their sins. This solemn prayer was followed by a time of rejoicing and celebration.

READ 1 KINGS 8

Prayer: *Lord, the joy, holiness, dignity, glory, and beauty that marked the early days of Solomon show what might have been had your people remained faithful to you. They also provide a hint of the far greater glory that is yet to be when you come to reign in righteousness. Thank you that you will reign again.*

Meditation passage for today: verses 27, 56

Day 94—1 Kings 9

After the dedication of the temple, the Lord appeared to Solomon a second time and exhorted him to walk before him in integrity of heart, uprightness, and obedience. The Lord made it clear that the temple was no talisman. He would destroy it if the people proved unfaithful to him.

Solomon's many construction projects required forced labor, and the Canaanites who remained in the land were enslaved for this purpose. Solomon also built a fleet of merchant ships and generated huge revenues through extensive foreign trade.

READ 1 KINGS 9

Prayer: *Lord, this passage teaches that there is a tension between the temporal and eternal value systems. Help me cling to you with a whole heart. I do not want my spiritual life to be choked by the cares of this world, the deceitfulness of riches, and the desires for other things.*

Meditation passage for today: verses 4–5

Day 95—1 Kings 10

According to the Abrahamic covenant, it was through Abraham's descendants that all the families of the earth would be blessed. This account of Solomon and the queen of Sheba illustrates how this was beginning to happen during the righteous portion of Solomon's reign.

When the queen came up to Jerusalem to test him with hard questions, Solomon's answers as well as the glory of his reign overwhelmed her. This was a rare instance in which reality exceeded the rumors. This woman left Jerusalem with praise for the God of Israel: "Blessed be the Lord your God who delighted in you to set you on the throne of Israel; because the Lord loved Israel forever, therefore he made you king, to do justice and righteousness." Solomon's fame and wealth continued to increase.

READ 1 KINGS 10

Prayer: *Lord, you intended the best for your covenant nation. How short-lived are the days of righteousness; we are prone to turn away from you in times of prosperity. Let me remember how fleeting are my days on this earth, so that I will not spend them in vain.*

Meditation passage for today: verse 9

Day 96—1 Kings 11

The tragic contrast between chapters 10 and 11 could not be greater. Up until this point, Solomon demonstrated a heart for the Lord, but the seeds of his own downfall were beginning to spread as he sought to multiply horses, wives, and wealth. This was in violation of the mandate for kings in Deuteronomy 17:14–20. Ironically, this wisest of men became a fool in his later years by succumbing to idolatry through the influence of his foreign wives.

When Solomon turned his heart away from the Lord to other gods, the Lord told him that he would tear the northern kingdom away from his progeny. In addition, the Lord began to raise up foreign adversaries against Solomon, and Solomon's servant Jeroboam also rebelled against him.

READ 1 KINGS 11

Prayer: *Lord, it is easy to see the seeds of destruction in the tragic story of Solomon. I ask that you would show me those subtle forces and patterns in my own life that could lead to my own downfall unless I remain faithful and cling to you.*

Meditation passage for today: verses 4, 9–10

Day 97—1 Kings 12

This chapter marks the transition in 931 B.C. from the united kingdom under Saul, David, and Solomon to the divided kingdom of Israel in the north (ten tribes) and Judah in the south (two tribes).

After the death of Solomon, his son Rehoboam foolishly rejected the prudent counsel of Jeroboam and the leaders of Israel to lighten the yoke his father had imposed upon the people. The court officials affirmed the reasonableness of this request. Instead, Rehoboam listened to the shallow counsel of his peers, who appealed to his pride. Rehoboam's harsh speech resulted in the revolt of the ten northern tribes, who made Jeroboam king over Israel. Sadly, Jeroboam set up an idolatrous rival religion in Israel, fearing that he would lose power if his people continued to worship at the temple in Jerusalem.

READ 1 KINGS 12

Prayer: *Lord, the devastating consequences of foolish pride are evident in the lives of Rehoboam and Jeroboam. I ask that out of your goodness you would make known to me, and take from my heart, every kind of pride.*

Meditation passage for today: verse 7

Day 98—1 Kings 17

In the days of Ahab, ruler of the northern kingdom of Israel, the Lord raised up the prophet Elijah to announce a drought because of Ahab's sin in bringing Baal worship to Israel through the influence of his wife Jezebel. The Lord provided for Elijah while he was in hiding by the brook Cherith, and then in the house of the widow Zarephath. The Lord miraculously replenished her flour and oil during the days of the drought and revived her dead son through Elijah's prayers. With the restoration of her son, Zarephath knew that Elijah was a man of God who spoke the true word of the Lord.

READ 1 KINGS 17

Prayer: *Lord, you provide for your people in the worst of circumstances and concern yourself with the details of our lives. May I trust you more and lean on you during times of trial and adversity.*

Meditation passage for today: verse 24

Day 99—1 Kings 18

When the Lord sent Elijah to Ahab to end the drought, Elijah encountered Obadiah and told him to announce Elijah's return to Ahab. Obadiah was a godly man who had protected and provided for one hundred prophets in two caves when Jezebel massacred the prophets of the Lord. However, he was afraid to tell Ahab until Elijah reassured him.

Ahab went to meet with Elijah, who challenged his false prophets to a contest on Mount Carmel. Elijah's dramatic single-handed victory over the 450 prophets of Baal and the four hundred prophets of Asherah led to the people's cry, "The Lord, he is God; the Lord, he is God." Then Elijah prayed on the top of Carmel for the drought-breaking rain.

READ 1 KINGS 18

Prayer: *Lord, I thank you for the boldness of your servant Elijah and for this remarkable account of your power on behalf of those whose lives are dedicated to you. May I grow in holy boldness and proclaim the truth of your Son in word and deed.*

Meditation passage for today: verses 21, 37

Day 100—1 Kings 19

Victory often produces vulnerability. After his spectacular public defeat of 850 false prophets, Elijah fled for his life when he received a threatening message from Queen Jezebel. In his depression and despair, Elijah was nourished by an angel as he headed south to Mount Horeb. There in a cave on the mountain, the Lord gently dealt with him. The Lord was not in the violent wind or the earthquake or the fire, but he spoke to Elijah in a still, small voice. The Lord instructed his despondent prophet to return north and anoint Hazael as king over Syria, Jehu as king over Israel, and Elisha as his successor.

READ 1 KINGS 19

Prayer: *Lord, I thank you for the gentle ways you encourage me in times of despondency. May I learn to fear and trust you rather than people, and may I have the courage to carry out your commands to the honor of your name.*

Meditation passage for today: verses 11–13, 18

Day 101—2 Kings 1

Ahaziah the son of Ahab followed the wicked ways of his father and continued the worship of Baal in Israel. When he was injured, the messengers he sent to inquire of the god Baal-Zebub were intercepted by Elijah, who sent them back to Ahaziah to tell him the Lord said he would die.

In his defiance, the king sent a band of soldiers to bring Elijah to him, but fire from heaven consumed them. This happened a second time, and the third group approached the prophet in humility and begged for their lives. Elijah went up with them and personally delivered the same message to Ahaziah, who soon died, in fulfillment of Elijah's word.

READ 2 KINGS 1

Prayer: *Lord, what you decree no one can change or thwart. You judge unrighteousness and arrogance and lift up the humble. Let me remember to treat you as holy and to walk before you in loving fear.*

Meditation passage for today: verse 16

Day 102—2 Kings 2

When Elijah knew the Lord was about to take him into heaven by a whirlwind, he discouraged his protégé Elisha from following him to Bethel and then to Jericho. Elisha refused to leave him, and the prophets in both places realized that the Lord was about to take his master away. Significantly, the waters of the Jordan River parted to allow Elijah and Elisha to cross on dry ground, and before Elijah was taken up into heaven, Elisha asked for a double portion of his spirit. Elisha took up the mantle of Elijah and parted the waters of the river. The prophets recognized that the spirit of Elijah rested on Elisha.

READ 2 KINGS 2

Prayer: *Lord, the way you took your servant Elijah up to heaven in a chariot of fire and a whirlwind reminds me of how little I really know about you. Your ways are truly mysterious. I also know that the things you are preparing for me are beyond my imagination, and that they will make the sufferings of this present life pale in comparison.*

Meditation passage for today: verses 9–12

Day 103—2 Kings 4

It is evident in this and the following chapters that Elisha indeed received a double portion of Elijah's spirit. There are many parallels between the miracles of Elisha and those of our Lord. The analogy has been made that Elijah is to Elisha as John the Baptist is to Jesus. Certainly the miracles of the increase of the widow's oil, the resuscitation of the Shunammite's son, the miracle of the deadly stew, and the multiplication of the loaves all foreshadow the miraculous ministry of the Lord Jesus. Elisha displayed compassion and concern for those around him and provided for their needs.

READ 2 KINGS 4

Prayer: *Lord, I am grateful for the ministry of Elisha and for the ways in which he typified Christ Jesus in his life and compassionate ministry. Thank you for the ways in which you have manifested your character and nature through your servants the prophets.*

Meditation passage for today: verses 37, 44

Day 104—2 Kings 5

When Naaman, commander of the army of the king of Syria, heard that there was a prophet in Israel who had the power to heal his leprosy, the king of Syria sent him with a letter to the king of Israel. The latter, however, thought such a request was the Syrian king's way of seeking a quarrel with him. Nevertheless, Elisha assured the Israelite king that he would deal with Naaman.

At first Naaman balked when told by Gehazi, Elisha's servant, to wash in the Jordan seven times, but he humbled himself, followed the instructions, and was cured. Sadly, Gehazi saw this as an opportunity for material gain, and because of his lie and his covetousness, he was struck with the leprosy of Naaman.

READ 2 KINGS 5

Prayer: *Lord, I thank you for this account of this Gentile's healing and conversion to you. I also thank you for the warning about the deceitfulness of the flesh and the lure of material gain. Let my character be free from covetousness so that I will be content with what I have.*

Meditation passage for today: verse 8

Day 105—2 Kings 6

Elisha continued to work signs and wonders. One of his gifts was the knowledge of what the enemies of Israel were plotting. When the king of Syria heard that Elisha was thwarting his plans, he sent an army to capture the prophet in Dothan. Elisha's servant was terrified to see the city surrounded, until Elisha prayed for him and he was granted a vision of God's protective forces. The Syrians were struck with blindness as Elisha led them to Samaria, Israel's capital, and then opened their eyes. But Elisha treated them with mercy and allowed them to return to Syria.

READ 2 KINGS 6

Prayer: *Lord, you empowered your prophet Elisha to accomplish great things. I thank you for the way you raise up choice servants for significant ministries to comfort and provide for your people. Please continue to work through your servants today.*

Meditation passage for today: verses 16–17

Day 106—2 Kings 7

During the Syrian siege of Samaria, the capital of Israel experienced such a severe famine that some of the people were resorting to cannibalism. The king of Israel blamed Elisha for the trouble and sought his life, but Elisha predicted that within one day the famine would end. When the Lord caused the Syrian army to hear the noise of a great army, they fled in terror, leaving their provisions behind. When four lepers decided to surrender to the Syrians rather than starve in Samaria, they were amazed to see the empty camp and all the goods. They announced the good news to the gatekeepers of Samaria, and after a cautious investigation proved it was true, the people of the city plundered the empty Syrian tents.

READ 2 KINGS 7

Prayer: *Lord, there are no circumstances so severe that they cannot be overturned in an instant if you choose to do so. May I look at you and your good pleasure rather than the circumstances I face, knowing that you will work all things together for good to those who love you and are called according to your purpose.*

Meditation passage for today: verses 6, 9

Day 107—2 Kings 8

Elisha warned the Shunammite woman whose son he had restored to life about a seven-year famine the Lord was about to bring. The family sojourned in the land of the Philistines, and Elisha's servant was instrumental in the restoration of their land after their return.

When Ben-Hadad, king of Syria, sent Hazael to Elisha to inquire if he would recover from his illness, Elisha told Hazael he would become king of Syria and ravage the children of Israel. The chapter concludes with an account of the wickedness of Joram, king of Israel, and Jehoram and Ahaziah, kings of Judah. In the ninth chapter, Elisha anoints as king over Israel Jehu, who executes both Joram and Ahaziah.

READ 2 KINGS 8

Prayer: *Lord, you are the sovereign Lord over history and the Judge of the rulers of the earth. Your Word reminds me that although the unrighteous reign for a season, the righteous will reign with Christ forever.*

Meditation passage for today: verses 11–13

Day 108—2 Kings 18

After the death of the ungodly King Ahaz of Judah, his son Hezekiah assumed the throne and provided a window of righteous rule in the southern kingdom until Hezekiah's wicked son Manasseh succeeded him. King Hezekiah zealously removed the high places and objects of pagan worship and walked in the ways of the Lord God of Israel.

It was in 722 B.C. during the reign of Hezekiah that the Assyrian King Shalmaneser finally overthrew the northern kingdom of Israel and scattered the people. After Hezekiah rebelled against the Assyrians, the Assyrian King Sennacherib sent forces to invade Judah, and Hezekiah relented by paying tribute. However, the Assyrians invaded Judah a second time and taunted Hezekiah for trusting in the God of Israel.

READ 2 KINGS 18

Prayer: *Lord, I know that there is no guarantee that righteousness will eliminate opposition and adversity in this life. Your enemies are ever active, but yours is the power, majesty, glory, and victory, and I will put my trust and hope in you.*

Meditation passage for today: verses 5–7

Day 109—2 Kings 19

When Hezekiah heard Assyria's taunts through Rabshakeh, he covered himself with sackcloth and went into the temple. He sent a contingent of men to ask Isaiah the prophet to pray for the remnant of Judah. Isaiah assured them that the Lord would respond to this blasphemy and prophesied the overthrow of Sennacherib and the Assyrian army. Then in one night, the angel of the Lord killed 185,000 of the Assyrian army that were surrounding Jerusalem. The defeated Sennacherib returned to Nineveh, where he was soon assassinated by two of his sons.

READ 2 KINGS 19

Prayer: *Lord, thank you for this account of Hezekiah's prayer, Isaiah's prophecy, and your sudden and mighty deliverance of your people in Jerusalem. Those who trust in you will overcome against impossible odds.*

Meditation passage for today: verses 15–16, 19

Day 110–2 Kings 20

When King Hezekiah was near death because of an illness, the prophet Isaiah told him he would not recover. But Hezekiah prayed to the Lord, and God instructed Isaiah to return and announce that he would grant the king an additional fifteen years of life. God gave Hezekiah a miraculous sign of his recovery, but not long after the king was healed, he foolishly and proudly displayed all of his treasures to a group of messengers from the king of Babylon. After he did this, Isaiah the prophet rebuked Hezekiah and prophesied that after his death, the Babylonians would carry away all of these treasures to their country.

READ 2 KINGS 20

Prayer: *Lord, even though you humbled Hezekiah through sickness, his heart succumbed to pride after he was cured. Please guard me from the subtle temptations to suppose that I can boast in anything other than you.*

Meditation passage for today: verses 5–6

Day 111—2 Kings 25

After a brief reform under Josiah, a succession of four ungodly rulers finally led to the demise of the kingdom of Judah. Nebuchadnezzar, king of Babylon, invaded Judah in 605 B.C. and again in 597 B.C., carrying off captives on both occasions. Nebuchadnezzar's third invasion, in 586 B.C., marked the end of the kingdom of Judah. Nebuzaradan, captain of the guard, finally destroyed the city of Jerusalem, tore down its walls, burned the temple and the palace, and carried away the bulk of the people into captivity in Babylon. The few remaining people eventually went down to Egypt for fear of the Chaldeans.

READ 2 KINGS 25

Prayer: *Lord, this sad story of the destruction of your temple is a powerful reminder of the bitter fruit of ungodliness. May I remain aware of the destructive consequences of disobedience to you and hold fast to you in humility, sincerity, and truth.*

Meditation passage for today: verses 8–11

Day 112—1 Chronicles 17

After David's kingdom was established, he began the construction of his palace and arranged to move the ark of the covenant up to the City of David in Jerusalem. He appointed an order of worship for the tabernacle and soon desired to build a permanent temple, where God would be worshiped and the ark of the covenant would be placed. The prophet Nathan told the king that the Lord would build David a lasting dynasty, and that David's son would be the one who would build the temple for the Lord. David responded in gratitude and praise for these covenant promises and asked that the Lord's name would be magnified through his descendants forever.

READ 1 CHRONICLES 17

Prayer: *Lord, I thank you for the promises of the Davidic covenant and for Jesus, the Root and the Offspring of David, who fulfills these covenant blessings. I thank you that Jesus will reign over the house of Jacob forever, and of his kingdom there will be no end.*

Meditation passage for today: verses 11–14, 20

Day 113—1 Chronicles 29

Chronicles gives a later priestly perspective on the period of the kings, and this is evident in the material in chapters 22 to 29. In this section of the book, detailed descriptions are given of the material provisions for the construction of the temple; the organization of the Levites and the priests; the orders of the temple musicians; the organization of the gatekeepers, the treasuries, and the temple officers; the leaders of the military divisions of Israel and of the twelve tribes; and the royal officers and counselors of David. The king gave his son Solomon the plans and provisions for the temple and offered a final prayer of thanksgiving before the coronation of his successor Solomon.

READ 1 CHRONICLES 29

Prayer: *Lord, the beauty, dignity, splendor, and order of Israel's worship at its peak in the reigns of David and Solomon were a great testimony to your grace and power. You transformed a people who were in bondage in Egypt and who wandered in the wilderness into a great and glorious nation.*

Meditation passage for today: verses 10–19

Day 114—2 Chronicles 34

Near the end of the southern kingdom, the Lord raised up a last godly king whose righteousness led his people for a few years into a time of reform, prosperity, and joy. Josiah was only sixteen when he began to seek the God of his forefather David. When he was twenty he began to purge Judah and Jerusalem of idolatrous images and altars.

At the age of twenty-six, Josiah ordered the repair of the house of God, and in the process, Hilkiah the high priest discovered the Book of the Law in the temple. When God's neglected Word was read to the king, Josiah realized that God's wrath must be great because of the years of neglect and disobedience. Sadly, Josiah's reforms would come too late to avert divine judgment on Judah.

READ 2 CHRONICLES 34

Prayer: *Lord, your Word became so neglected by your people that it was lost for years. I ask that I will never take your Word for granted, but that I will remain faithful to the disciplines of reading and meditating on Scripture.*

Meditation passage for today: verses 21, 33

Day 115—2 Chronicles 35

In his response to the reading of the Book of the Law of Moses, King Josiah commanded that the people celebrate the Passover to the Lord for the first time in years. This was the greatest celebration of the Passover since the days of Samuel the prophet.

Josiah was a capable leader whose passion for the Lord and commitment to him were contagious. He was able to rally the priests and the Levites and all Judah and Israel who were present. During his days, the people followed his direction by committing themselves to the Lord, but after his death, these reforms were quickly abandoned. The people fell under the sway of a succession of four godless kings who brought the kingdom of Judah to ruin.

READ 2 CHRONICLES 35

Prayer: *Lord, Josiah's reign brought a brief interlude of righteousness that showed what might have been had your people remained faithful to you. Seeking their own interests above yours, they brought about their own destruction. May I be careful to seek your interests first.*

Meditation passage for today: verses 16–18

Day 116—Ezra 1

The Book of Ezra contains the stories of the first two returns of the Jewish exiles at the conclusion of the Babylonian captivity. Ezra 1–6 portrays the first return, led by Zerubbabel, and the construction of the second temple in Jerusalem (538–516 B.C.). Ezra 7–10 presents the second return, led by Ezra, and the reformation of the people under his leadership (458–457 B.C.). With the decree of Cyrus, king of Persia (559–530 B.C.), the Jewish people were granted permission to return to their land and to rebuild the house of the Lord in Jerusalem. Moreover, Cyrus returned the temple articles that had been taken by the Babylonians so that the captives could use them in the new temple.

READ EZRA 1

Prayer: *Lord, you are sovereign over the empires of this earth, and you use their rulers to accomplish your purposes. I thank you that you never abandoned your people but preserved a remnant who could return to the land and continue the messianic line.*

Meditation passage for today: verses 2–3

Day 117—Ezra 3

In spite of fear of reprisal, Jeshua and Zerubbabel gathered the remnant and built the altar of the God of Israel so that the people could once again offer sacrifices to the Lord. They also celebrated the Feast of Tabernacles and began work on the foundation of the second temple in accordance with the decree issued by Cyrus, king of Persia.

When the builders completed the temple foundation, the priests celebrated with instruments and music to praise the Lord, singing responsively, "For he is good, for his loving-kindness is upon Israel forever." However, the shouts of joy were mingled with weeping by the older people who could remember the greater glory of the first temple.

READ EZRA 3

Prayer: *Lord, your covenant faithfulness to your people is great, and your mercies never cease. However, this text reminds us of the long-term consequences of disobedience. Still you promise that by your grace, the best is yet to come.*

Meditation passage for today: verse 11

Day 118—Ezra 4

The adversaries of Judah and Benjamin sought to discourage work on the new temple, but under the firm leadership of Zerubbabel and Jeshua God's people tried to continue. However, their opponents were persistent, and this ongoing problem of attempting to prevent the Jewish people from being well-established in the land continued. This is evident in the account in the second part of Ezra 4. There was later opposition under Artaxerxes, king of Persia (464–423 B.C.), when the Jews first attempted to rebuild the walls of Jerusalem. The opponents of the Jewish people sent an alarming letter to Artaxerxes, who responded by instructing them to make the Jews cease their work on the walls. The chapter ends by bringing us back to the time of Zerubbabel and the discontinuation of the work on the temple.

READ EZRA 4

Prayer: *Lord, it is not always clear to us why you allow godless agendas and spiritual warfare to delay your work in this world, but I know that I can always trust you for the outcome, no matter how difficult the journey may seem.*

Meditation passage for today: verse 3

Day 119—Ezra 5

The second temple was begun under Zerubbabel's leadership in 536 B.C., discontinued in 534 B.C., and not resumed until 520 B.C., when the prophets Haggai and Zechariah exhorted the Jewish people to complete the temple. Inspired by these prophets, Zerubbabel and Jeshua resumed the work. Immediately their opponents challenged them and asked them who gave them the right to resume. They refused to cease unless Darius, king of Persia (521–486 B.C.), issued an edict to this effect. When the opponents of the Jews wrote to Darius, they referred to the Jewish claim that Cyrus had issued a decree to build the temple and asked that a search be made for such a decree.

READ EZRA 5

Prayer: *Lord, the pressures of this world often discourage your people from pressing on in obedience. May I remember that all who desire to live godly in Christ Jesus will suffer persecution. May I take courage, knowing that you have overcome the world.*

Meditation passage for today: verses 5, 11

Day 120—Ezra 6

King Darius responded to the letter sent by the opponents of the temple construction by ordering that a search be made in the archives for the alleged decree of Cyrus that the Jews build their temple. Providentially, a scroll was found that contained this decree, and this led Darius to command that the very people who opposed the temple construction assist in providing the means for its completion. Thus encouraged by this decree and the prophetic ministry of Haggai and Zechariah, the children of Israel completed their temple in 516 B.C. They joyfully celebrated the dedication of the temple and later celebrated the Passover at the new house of God in Jerusalem.

READ EZRA 6

Prayer: *Lord, you use even your opponents to accomplish your good pleasure. I thank you that you provide for your people through unexpected means and that we can confidently look to you rather than fear opposition.*

Meditation passage for today: verses 10, 16, 22

Day 121—Nehemiah 1

The Book of Nehemiah records the third return of the Jews from Babylonian captivity, led by Nehemiah (444–425 B.C.). While Zerubbabel, Haggai, and Zechariah had been concerned with the building of the second temple, decades later Nehemiah focused on the rebuilding of the walls around the city of Jerusalem, where the temple was located. Some years earlier, the Jews evidently had rebuilt most of the walls of Jerusalem (see Ezr 4:6–23), but Nehemiah was distressed to hear that they had been broken down and the gates burned. Nehemiah responded by interceding for his people in their plight.

READ NEHEMIAH 1

Prayer: *Lord, you are the great and awesome God who hears the cries of your people and grants us grace rather than retribution. I thank you that I can boldly approach the throne of grace to obtain mercy and find grace to help in time of need.*

Meditation passage for today: verses 5–6, 10–11

Day 122—Nehemiah 2

Nehemiah served as the cupbearer to Artaxerxes, king of Persia (464–423 B.C.), and it was in the twentieth year of Artaxerxes (444 B.C.) that Nehemiah heard the disturbing news that the walls of Jerusalem had been reduced to rubble. His sorrow was evident to the king, and when Artaxerxes heard the cause of Nehemiah's concern, he invited him to make his request. Nehemiah was prepared, and he presented a clear plan of action to the king. He journeyed to Jerusalem with men and provisions, inspected the walls of the city, and encouraged its inhabitants to begin the good work of rebuilding. Nehemiah also refuted the accusations of the enemies of the children of Israel.

READ NEHEMIAH 2

Prayer: *Lord, I am grateful for the godly example of Nehemiah, who had a passion for your purposes and for the plight of your people. Give me a heart that seeks to be pleasing to you and the courage to set my hands to your good work.*

Meditation passage for today: verses 4, 18

Day 123—Nehemiah 4

Under Nehemiah's leadership, the people of Jerusalem began the construction of the city wall, with each group working in the area of their habitation. Seeing this, their enemies Sanballat and Tobiah sought to dishearten the people by mocking their efforts, but Nehemiah prayed and encouraged the people to continue.

Alarmed at the progress of the work, their enemies plotted to attack and confuse the Jews, but Nehemiah prayed, put them in readiness, and encouraged them to continue. Half of the people stood watch while the other half continued the construction, and in this way they continued to progress without being intimidated by the threats of their enemies.

READ NEHEMIAH 4

Prayer: *Lord, I thank you for the balance of dependence and diligence illustrated in this chapter and for the godly leadership of Nehemiah, who encouraged, exhorted, and equipped the people to continue the good work to which you called them. May I also press on in your calling and stand firm in you during spiritual warfare.*

Meditation passage for today: verses 9, 14

Day 124—Nehemiah 5

Not only did the Jews experience external opposition from their enemies, but they were also suffering from internal oppression by their nobles and rulers. Hearing that many of the people were being forced into servitude by those who were exacting usury, Nehemiah rebuked these manipulators. He required them to return the interest and stop abusing their brethren. Nehemiah also became an example to these nobles by refusing to take his rightful governor's provisions—instead, he shared with those who were in need.

READ NEHEMIAH 5

Prayer: *Lord, I know that opposition to your calling in my life comes not only from without but also from within. I ask that you would reveal any selfish and manipulative strategies that I have been guilty of following and set me free as I set my heart on your Son.*

Meditation passage for today: verses 9, 19

Day 125—Nehemiah 6

As the work on the walls continued to progress, the enemies of the Jews continued to conspire to keep Jerusalem from being fortified. Sanballat, Tobiah, Geshem, and others sought to trick Nehemiah into leaving the work to meet with them so they could do him harm. Nehemiah wisely ignored their multiple messages, and he denied their false charges that he was fortifying the city to set himself up as king. Their next ploy was more subtle: they hired Shemaiah to pose as a prophet of the Lord to get Nehemiah to hide himself in the temple. Nehemiah strengthened himself in the Lord and refused to succumb to intimidation. The walls were completed in only fifty-two days, evidence that the hand of God was upon them.

READ NEHEMIAH 6

Prayer: *Lord, thank you for the reminder that I too am engaged in spiritual warfare between the forces of good and evil. I must be ever vigilant and dependent upon you. I will declare Christ as Lord in my heart and not be intimidated or fearful.*

Meditation passage for today: verse 16

Day 126—Nehemiah 8

After the construction of the walls of Jerusalem, it was necessary to consecrate and consolidate the people. Just as Ezra the priest had led reforms thirteen years earlier (see Ezr 9-10), now he led the children of Israel in a time of spiritual renewal as they recommitted themselves to their covenant with God (444 B.C.).

Standing on a special platform that was built for the purpose, Ezra brought the Book of the Law, blessed the Lord, and read it to the congregation that gathered together to hear it. When the people heard God's Word, they wept in remorse, but Nehemiah the governor encouraged them to take strength in the joy of the Lord. The people responded to the Law by keeping the Feast of Booths for seven days as they continued to listen to the Book of the Law of God.

READ NEHEMIAH 8

Prayer: *Lord, I thank you for your Word and that it is readily available. May I realize that the joy of the Lord is my strength and expose myself to your truth each day with a heart of obedience.*

Meditation passage for today: verses 10-11

Day 127—Nehemiah 9

When the children of Israel gathered for a national day of fasting and penance, they heard a reading from the Book of the Law and responded with a period of confession and worship. Their spiritual leaders guided them through a beautiful and powerful psalm of praise for the great deliverances of the Lord.

This psalm recalls many things, including the work of God in creation, the calling and covenant with Abram, the deliverance of Israel from Egypt through the Red Sea, the giving of the Law on Mount Sinai, the rebellion of the people in the wilderness, the faithful provision of God, the conquest of the land, the kingdom, Israel's unfaithfulness and consequent captivity, and a plea for restoration.

READ NEHEMIAH 9

Prayer: *Lord, you have always proven yourself faithful to your people in spite of our unfaithfulness and rebelliousness. May I remember your many good works on my behalf and cling to you. Fill me with your Holy Spirit so that I will walk in your grace and power.*

Meditation passage for today: verses 6, 17, 31

Day 128—Esther 1

The Book of Esther takes place in 483–473 B.C. during the reign of Ahasuerus, king of Persia (486–464 B.C.). Although the name of God does not appear in this book, his sovereign protection of his people who were scattered in the provinces of Persia is evident in its pages.

When Ahasuerus (known to the Greeks as Xerxes) made a feast for the many officials of the Medo–Persian Empire, he displayed his opulence and served wine in abundance. Queen Vashti also made a feast for the women, but when Ahasuerus sent for Vashti to come and display her beauty to the officials, she refused to obey. The king's counselors advised him to depose her to set an example throughout the empire that "every man should be the master in his own house."

READ ESTHER 1

Prayer: *Lord, I am reminded that the wealth and pomp of this world is fleeting and unsatisfying. Only those who find their identity and hope in you will enjoy true security, significance, and satisfaction.*

Meditation passage for today: verse 4

Day 129—Esther 2

When Ahasuerus' servants advised him to appoint officers throughout his kingdom who would search for beautiful virgins to gather to Shushan, the king was pleased with the idea of selecting one of these women to replace his former queen. One of the women who was taken to the king's palace was Esther, a Jewish girl who had been raised by her relative Mordecai. While Esther was being prepared with the other virgins to see the king, she concealed her Jewish identity. When her turn came, this gracious and beautiful woman won the favor of Ahasuerus, who had her crowned as his new queen.

Later, Mordecai warned Esther about a plot to assassinate the king, and she informed the king in Mordecai's name. The report was confirmed, the conspirators were hanged, and it was written in the court chronicles.

READ ESTHER 2

Prayer: *Lord, you sovereignly work in human affairs and use unknown, humble people to accomplish extraordinary things. Just as you chose this young woman to accomplish your purposes, I ask that you would let me participate in your purposes as well.*

Meditation passage for today: verses 17, 20

Day 130—Esther 3

Ahasuerus' appointment of the arrogant Haman to the role of prime minister meant trouble for the Jews when Mordecai refused to bow or pay homage to him. When Haman heard of it and learned that Mordecai was a Jew, he plotted to destroy every Jew throughout the Persian Empire. He asked the king to allow him to draw up a royal decree to eliminate the Jews from every province on a day he had determined by casting Pur (the lot). When the decree was copied and sent by courier throughout the many provinces of the empire, it caused consternation among all the Jewish people who heard of it.

READ ESTHER 3

Prayer: *Lord, the rage and malice of Haman shows the ugliness and destructive nature of human pride. I realize that pride can cause me to react in ways that are utterly disproportionate to an offense, and I ask that you would protect me from the folly of self-promotion and arrogance.*

Meditation passage for today: verse 4

Day 131—Esther 4

When the Jews heard of the decree for their elimination, they cried out and mourned with fasting and sack-cloth. When Esther heard Mordecai was wearing sackcloth, she sent Hathach, one of her attendants, to learn why he was mourning. He gave Hathach a copy of the decree and told him to request that the queen make intercession for her people. Esther responded that to go before the king uninvited would be to risk her life. Mordecai sent word that her life would be forfeit with the rest of the Jews if she did not. Esther agreed to go to the king after the Jews in the city fasted three days for her.

READ ESTHER 4

Prayer: *Lord, you sovereignly orchestrate opportunities for your people to participate in doing your will on this earth. I ask that I would have the insight and courage to lay hold of the opportunities you bring so that I will not miss out on your intentions for me.*

Meditation passage for today: verses 13–14

Day 132—Esther 5

After fasting for three days, Esther prepared to go before the king. When he saw her in the court, he favorably raised the golden scepter and invited her to approach. Asked to make a request, she invited the king and Haman to a private banquet. At the banquet, the king again invited her to make a request, and Esther asked them to come to another banquet on the following day, when she would reveal her request. Haman was delighted with the apparent favor he was receiving, and he proudly recounted his position and privileges to his friends. When Haman said that all this was sullied by the disrespect of Mordecai, his wife suggested he have a gallows built and ask the king to have Mordecai hanged on it.

READ ESTHER 5

Prayer: *Lord, I thank you for the wisdom of Esther in contrast to the folly of Haman. May I seek the grace of humility and dependence upon you rather than the folly of arrogance and independence.*

Meditation passage for today: verse 8

Day 133—Esther 6

When the king providentially heard the account of how Mordecai had averted an assassination attempt, he wanted him to be rewarded. Ironically, at that moment Haman was at court to ask the king to hang Mordecai. When the king asked Haman what should be done for the man the king wished to honor, Haman proudly assumed the king meant him and answered accordingly.

To his horror, Haman discovered the king intended this honor for Mordecai the Jew and that he should bring it about. When Haman told his wife and friends what had happened, they realized he was about to fall before Mordecai. Just then, the king's eunuchs arrived to take Haman to Esther's banquet.

READ ESTHER 6

Prayer: *Lord, the rich irony and plot twists of this book display the truth of Mary's words in Luke 1: "He has scattered those who were proud in the thoughts of their heart. He has brought down rulers from their thrones and has exalted those who were humble."*

Meditation passage for today: verse 13

Day 134—Esther 7

When the king and Haman went to Esther's second banquet, the king asked Esther to name her request. She then revealed her Jewish identity to the king and pled for the lives of her people. When the king asked who would presume to kill her and her people, the queen accused Haman of the deed. Haman was terrified, and when the king went out in anger to the palace garden, Haman fell across Esther's couch, pleading for his life. When the king returned and saw this, the guard covered Haman's face. At the suggestion of one of the eunuchs, the king ordered Haman to be hanged on the very gallows he had prepared for Mordecai.

READ ESTHER 7

Prayer: *Lord, I thank you for this story about a woman who wisely discerned the fitting time and place to intercede on behalf of the Jewish people. May I also act in accordance with your timing, your way, and your power.*

Meditation passage for today: verse 3

Day 135—Esther 8

Yet another irony in this book is the fact that Mordecai was given the house of Haman, the deceased enemy of the Jews. Esther sought to reverse the decree that Haman had deceitfully carried out in the name of the king. Since the former decree could not be revoked, the king granted Esther and Mordecai the right to issue another royal decree that would counteract the decree engineered by Haman. They acted quickly and arranged for the new decree to be carried throughout the provinces of the empire, which permitted the Jews to avenge themselves on those who would assault them. "For the Jews there was light and gladness and joy and honor."

READ ESTHER 8

Prayer: *Lord, thank you that you hear the prayers of those who cry out to you and honor those who seek to honor you. In your sovereignty, you even use the evil counsels of men to accomplish your will, and nothing can thwart your loving purposes for your people.*

Meditation passage for today: verse 16

Day 136—Esther 9

On the day appointed for their destruction, the Jews through-out the provinces gathered and overpowered their enemies instead. Fear of them fell upon all the people, and they were able to defeat their adversaries. In the capital city of Shushan, the Jews killed five hundred enemies, including the ten sons of Haman. Esther requested that her people in Shushan be granted an additional day to defeat their opponents, and this was carried out. To commemorate their deliverance and victory, Mordecai and Esther decreed that the Jews celebrate an annual feast of Purim, named after Pur, the lot Haman had cast to fix the date for his decree to be enacted.

READ ESTHER 9

Prayer: *Lord, you transform our sorrow into joy, and our travail into laughter. Thank you for this beautiful portrait of your subtle but sovereign work. Help me remember the bigger picture of your power and grace so I will abide in hope in times of adversity.*

Meditation passage for today: verses 17, 22

Day 137—Job 1

The Book of Job, evidently set around the time of the patri-arch Abraham, teaches that God is sovereign over all things. It shows that God is worthy of our worship even when we do not understand what he is doing in our lives. Job was such a godly man that the Lord used him as an example to the Adversary, who promptly asserted that Job worshiped God only for his benefits, not for himself. When God gave Satan permission to take away Job's material blessings, Job responded to the series of calamities by honoring God rather than charging the Lord with wrong.

READ JOB 1

Prayer: *Lord, I am amazed at the faith of your servant Job, who trusted you enough to hold fast to your good character in spite of his devastating circumstances. Please give me the grace to depend upon you and trust you in all things, especially when I don't understand what is happening.*

Meditation passage for today: verse 21

Day 138—Job 2

When Satan presented himself once again before the Lord, God affirmed Job's continued blamelessness in spite of Satan's heinous work of bringing disaster on Job's possessions and children. The Adversary pressed his previous claim that Job still served God because of his benefits, and he pointed to Job's physical health. This time, the Lord allowed Satan to attack Job's person but not to take his life. Satan immediately struck Job with painful boils all over his body, so that the pain was excruciating and unabated. Now reduced to nothing, Job still maintained his integrity and renounced his wife's advice to "Curse God and die!" When Job's three friends came to comfort him, they did not recognize him.

READ JOB 2

Prayer: *Lord, I can only wonder how I would respond under such adverse circumstances as these. Yet I know that other saints besides Job have endured as much and held fast to you. I ask for a heart of gratitude for your many benefits and tender mercies, as well as a heart that loves you above all these.*

Meditation passage for today: verse 10

Day 139—Job 38

The Book of Job records three cycles of debate between Job and his friends (first cycle: 3–14; second cycle: 15–21; third cycle: 22–26). The cycles increase in emotional intensity as Eliphaz, Bildad, and Zophar claim that Job is suffering because of his sins, while Job defends his innocence with growing vehemence. Job's responses, including his closing monologue (27–31) become increasingly self-righteous as he accuses God of not listening to him and of unjustly punishing him while allowing the wicked to prosper. Elihu finally speaks and urges Job to humble himself while God purifies him through the trials he is experiencing (32–37). The Lord himself ends the debate by speaking to Job of his power and wisdom in creating and sustaining the world and all its creatures (38–39).

READ JOB 38

Prayer: *Lord, I realize that I am too nearsighted to understand what you are doing, and I know that sometimes there is no explanation for our suffering. Let me understand that you are more concerned that I trust you than that I understand you, since your ways exceed my own.*

Meditation passage for today: verses 2–7

Day 140—Job 39

Using a series of questions about the glories and wonders of his manifold and varied creation, the Lord taught Job that God alone is in control of the created order. In chapters 38–39, the Lord referred to the earth, the sea, the sun, the snow and hail, the wind and rain, the stars, lions, mountain goats, wild donkeys, the wild ox, the ostrich, the horse, the hawk, and the eagle. Each of these wonders reflects the handiwork of God and transcends human wisdom and power. Through these questions, the Lord reminded Job of his frailty, finitude, and need to turn from his own wisdom to that of the omnipotent and infinite Lord of all creation.

READ JOB 39

Prayer: *Lord, when I reflect on the multitude of mysteries that surround me, I realize how foolish it is for me to question your ways and doubt that you are in sovereign control. If you order the cosmos, I can surely trust you to order my life.*

Meditation passage for today: verses 1, 5, 9, 19, 26–27

Day 141—Job 40

After the Lord's round of questions, Job responded by acknowledging his insignificance and presumption. He realized that he had spoken about things of which he has no knowledge, and that his attempts to contend with the Almighty were born out of foolishness. But the Lord wanted Job to see more than this. In a second speech to Job, he illustrated his ability to control all things (40–41). The Lord told Job that he would need to have the power of the Almighty to contend with him. He illustrated this power and authority in describing two of his many creatures. The first is the behemoth, and this Hebrew word appears only in Job 40:15. This awesome creature is only one of the manifold works of God.

READ JOB 40

Prayer: *Lord, forgive me for the presumption with which I grumble about my circumstances and indirectly accuse you of mismanagement. Thank you for this reminder that you alone are in sovereign control of all things, and that I cannot control even a day of my life.*

Meditation passage for today: verses 6–14

Day 142—Job 41

After his poetic description of the behemoth, the Lord vividly described another of his many creatures to illustrate his sovereignty over the entire created order and his ability to control the uncontrollable. As with the behemoth in Job 40, the leviathan in Job 41 is not easily identified. Judging from the poetic images of the leviathan's strength and size, plus the other biblical passages that mention this creature, this appears to be a large sea creature. While it has been suggested that the behemoth is a hippopotamus and leviathan is a crocodile, others think the descriptions in Job 40–41 seem to describe creatures that are larger and more powerful, even taking poetic exaggeration into account.

READ JOB 41

Prayer: *Lord, your creation, with its rich array of extinct and existing animals and plants, abounds with marvels and wonders. Any one of these living things displays an elegance and complexity that greatly transcends our most advanced technology. May I always be more impressed by your world than by the realm of human achievements.*

Meditation passage for today: verses 1–5, 33–34

Day 143—Job 42

Job's response to God in 40:3–5 was a realization of his fini-tude and presumption, but here in 42:1–6 he responds in humility and repentance. His direct encounter with the awe-some God of all creation brings him to the point of contrition for his self-righteousness, which had been growing through the course of his debates with his friends. The real issue in Job is not suffering but sovereignty. The lesson Job ultimately learned through the things he suffered is that God alone is in sovereign control of all things. When Job prayed for his three friends, the Lord doubled what he had lost and gave him children to replace those he had taken away.

READ JOB 42

Prayer: *Lord, I am grateful that you care for your people and teach us the painful lessons we need to receive. You always intend good for us in the end, and you are compassionate and merciful.*

Meditation passage for today: verses 1–6

Day 144—Psalm 1

The Psalter, comprising five books in one, powerfully and beautifully portrays the whole range of human emotions. It has served as the most comforting and relevant book of the Bible for generations of believers. The psalms show us how to praise and worship God both in good and in difficult times. They call us to put our hope in God and not in people or resources.

The first psalm is a fitting doorkeeper to the Psalter as a whole because of its stark contrast between the way of life and the way of death. It begins with a negative and positive description of the person who is blessed in the sight of God. This sharply contrasts with the fate of those who have rejected God's claims on their lives.

READ PSALM 1

Prayer: *Lord, I thank you for this clear reminder that those who delight in and meditate on your instructions for living will grow and bear the fruit of character and joy. May I be responsive to your Word and delight in it.*

Meditation passage for today: verses 2–3

Day 145—Psalm 19

This psalm begins with a poetic description of God's general revelation in the world of nature (verses 1–6). Although we do not hear the sun and the stars, they speak with eloquence about the greatness and glory of God. The second part of the psalm is a hymn extolling the riches of the Lord's special revelation through his Word (verses 7–10).

The six facets of the diamond of the Torah (law, testimony, precepts, commandment, fear, and judgments) refract the dazzling light of God's goodness and grace. The psalm concludes with a personal response to God's revelation in the world and the Word (verses 11–14). David expresses his intention to follow the way of God in his actions and attitudes.

READ PSALM 19

Prayer: *Lord, I marvel at your greatness, glory, goodness, and grace. Your revelation in creation and in your Word reveals your glorious attributes and invites me to respond to your loving overtures. Help me to follow your ways.*

Meditation passage for today: verses 1, 7–11

Day 146—Psalm 23

The best known of all the psalms is a brief but marvelous meditation by a shepherd who draws an analogy between his caring relationship with his flock and the Lord's care for him. This psalm poetically presents the ongoing goodness and mercy of the Lord throughout the life of his sheep. In the first two verses, David portrays the Lord as a shepherd who loves and cares for his flock. In the next two verses, the Lord is envisioned as a shepherd who guides and protects his sheep. The last two verses describe God as a shepherd who provides for and abides with his flock.

READ PSALM 23

Prayer: *Lord, I thank you that I have become a member of your flock through faith in Christ Jesus. Your presence will be my joy forever. May I become accustomed to practicing your presence during the brief years of my earthly sojourn.*

Meditation passage for today: verses 1–6

Day 147—Psalm 32

Psalm 32 is one of the seven "penitential psalms" (the others are Psalms 6, 38, 51, 102, 130, and 143). It records the anguish and subsequent deliverance of a man who sought to deny and cover up his guilt before the holy eyes of God. The psalm opens with a joyful word about the blessing of forgiveness (verses 1–2). In verses 3–5, David recalls the painful effects of his stubbornness and the turning point of his repentance. The wisdom of repentance is evident in the conclusion of the psalm. Those who do not know the Lord and believers who refuse to be honest with him will try to cover up or rationalize their transgressions. Only when we turn to him or turn back to him can we know the liberation and blessing of forgiveness and newness of life.

READ PSALM 32

Prayer: *Lord, thank you for instructing me and teaching me in the way I should go, and that your mercy surrounds me when I trust in you. May I be glad in the Lord and rejoice in your forgiveness.*

Meditation passage for today: verses 1–2, 6–8

Day 148—Psalm 37

Psalm 37 is a wisdom psalm that instructs us in the importance of maintaining the right perspective during our earthly journey. It is a beautifully crafted acrostic poem that begins almost every other verse with each successive letter of the Hebrew alphabet. Like the Book of Proverbs, this instructional poem contains wisdom sayings that encourage us to take the long view of life and see things from an eternal perspective. The bulk of this psalm contrasts the pursuits and the destiny of the wicked and the righteous. It grants that for a while those who refuse to acknowledge God may prosper, while those who seek God often suffer at the hands of evildoers. Ultimately, the righteous will endure and inherit the land.

READ PSALM 37

Prayer: *Lord, by your grace I want to trust in you, to delight myself in you, to commit my way to you, and to be still and wait patiently for you. Thank you that I can rest in you and in this way overcome the concerns that would make me anxious.*

Meditation passage for today: verses 3–7, 23–24, 39–40

Day 149—Psalm 73

Psalm 73 is the record of Asaph's struggle with the issue of why good things happen to bad people and why bad things happen to good people. Asaph begins his meditation with an affirmation of the goodness of God but honestly admits that he went through a crisis of faith in which he questioned the truth of this affirmation.

Contrary to the prosperity gospel, there is no assurance that obedience to God will lead to material or physical well-being. When Asaph went to the temple to bring his affliction before the Lord, his perspective was radically changed. The turning point in the psalm is reached when the author takes his eyes away from the foolish pride of people and turns them to the glory and counsel of God.

READ PSALM 73

Prayer: *Lord, may I repent of the bitterness of heart that comes from putting my hope in anything other than your goodness and promises. May I long for the things you declare to be important and live in the goodness of drawing near to you.*

Meditation passage for today: verses 23–28

Day 150—Psalm 90

This "prayer of Moses, the man of God" is the oldest of the 150 psalms in the biblical Psalter. This thoughtful and poignant meditation on the brevity of human life was written almost 3,400 years ago. Scholars place it near the end of the wilderness wanderings of the children of Israel, when Moses was in his final years.

In spite of its antiquity, the message of this psalm speaks to our time with particular relevance and force. It begins with a brilliant contrast between the eternalness of God and the brevity of human existence on earth. The pivotal verse asks the Lord to "teach us to number our days, that we may present to you a heart of wisdom" (verse 12). This psalm invites us to embrace an eternal perspective in a temporal world.

READ PSALM 90

Prayer: *Lord, teach me to number my days aright. May I make the decision each day to be defined by the eternal so that I will not be defined by the temporal world system.*

Meditation passage for today: verses 1–2, 12, 17

Day 151—Psalm 103

Psalm 103 begins a group of psalms of praise (Psalms 103–107), which remind us with skill and beauty that God's lovingkindness is the source of our greatest satisfaction.

The psalm begins with a personal hymn of thanksgiving (verses 1–5) in which David recounts several reasons to praise the Lord based on his personal experience of walking with him. The psalm shifts in the second stanza from an individual thanksgiving to a communal hymn of praise around the theme of God's loyal love (verses 6–18). The third stanza of the psalm transports us from the individual and the community to the entire created order (verses 19–22). The meditation moves from God's grace to God's greatness as the psalmist invokes the myriad angelic and heavenly hosts to bless God's holy name.

READ PSALM 103

Prayer: *Lord, if I do not love you with my whole being, I will love some lesser good with my whole being. I ask that I would put you first in my affections and seek you as my supreme good and final joy.*

Meditation passage for today: verses 1–5, 8, 11–13

Day 152—Psalm 104

This beautiful hymn of praise explores the entire created order as a testimony to the glory of God and his wonderful works on every level from the great to the small. It begins with the majesty of God himself and journeys from the heavens to the earth. The psalmist considers the large-scale features of the earth's atmosphere, oceans, and land masses, then focuses in on the rich variety of creatures that inhabit this planet, including wild donkeys, birds, wild goats, rock badgers, lions, and sea creatures. Everything comes from the hand of the Lord, and it is he who sustains all living systems. When God's people meditate on the creation, they renew their appreciation for his greatness and glory.

READ PSALM 104

Prayer: *Lord, may your glory endure forever. Praise you for all of your wondrous creation. All that we have comes from you. Thank you for providing for our needs.*

Meditation passage for today: verses 1–2, 24, 31

Day 153—Psalm 107

Psalm 107 is a resource that encourages us to keep a grateful memory alive by remembering God's benefits in the past. The psalmist creates four different scenes to depict the return of the Israelites from Babylonian captivity. Each scene uses the same refrain of thanksgiving: "Let them give thanks to the Lord for his lovingkindness, and for his wonders to the sons of men!" All four scenes reveal the folly of thinking we are masters of our fate. We would be wise to recognize ourselves in the fourfold picture of plight and salvation: *we* are the wanderers, the prisoners, the sick, and the storm-tossed who have been retrieved, released, restored, and rescued.

READ PSALM 107

Prayer: *Lord, in your severe mercy you sometimes take me to the end of my rope, but you are always faithful to those who cling to you during the tough times of life. May I cultivate an ongoing attitude of gratitude by remembering the good things you have done for me.*

Meditation passage for today: verses 1, 8, 43

Day 154—Psalm 139

There is no higher calling than to love and worship the infinite and personal God of creation and redemption. In complete contrast to the world, God's economy measures greatness not in terms of ability or accomplishments but in the vitality and integrity of a person's walk with the Lord.

This meditation on the Person and works of God reveals the depth of David's relationship with God. Its four stanzas are reflections on the attributes of God: God is all-knowing (verses 1–6), all-present (verses 7–12), all-powerful (verses 13–18), and all-holy (verses 19–24). God knows us intimately and is present with us in any adversity we face.

READ PSALM 139

Prayer: *Lord, I ask with David that you would search me and know my heart, try me and know my anxious thoughts, see if there be any hurtful way in me, and lead me in the everlasting way.*

Meditation passage for today: verses 1–3, 14, 23–24

Day 155—Psalm 145

Psalm 145, the last of the Davidic psalms, is a skillfully constructed acrostic poem. The psalm invites the people of God to let their spirits resonate with his Spirit as it alternates calls to praise and reasons for praise. It begins with the unsearchable greatness of God (verses 1–8) and the glorious splendor of his majesty. The psalm then moves to the theme of the goodness of God (verses 9–13) and his tender mercies that are over all his works. David concludes with a meditation on the grace of God (verses 14–21) and the way he fulfills the desire of those who call upon him and fear him.

READ PSALM 145

Prayer: *Lord, I will extol you, my God, O King, and I will bless your name forever and ever. You are great and highly to be praised, and your greatness is unsearchable. All your works shall give thanks to you, O Lord, and your godly ones shall bless you.*

Meditation passage for today: verses 1–3, 5, 8, 17–21

Day 156—Proverbs 1

Proverbs is an immensely practical and specific book that challenges us to pursue wisdom in each area of everyday life. It counsels us to depend upon God and order our ways before him in our relationships with our wives or husbands, children, work, friends, and neighbors. It encourages us to develop a godly character that will become evident in our speech, our use of money and time, and the decisions we make.

The purpose of Proverbs is expressly given in 1:2-6. This book was collected first to impart moral insight and astuteness (1:2a, 3-5), and second to help the reader develop mental ability and understanding (1:2b, 6). The theme of this book is captured in 1:7: "The fear of the Lord is the beginning of knowledge; fools despise wisdom and instruction."

READ PROVERBS 1

Prayer: *Lord, may I respond to wisdom's call and avoid the enticement of folly. I want to receive the instruction of wisdom, justice, judgment, and equity so that I will walk in prudence and discernment.*

Meditation passage for today: verses 2-7

Day 157—Proverbs 2

The Book of Proverbs begins by preparing the reader to receive instruction (verses 1-9). A clear statement of the purpose of the book (1:1-7) is followed by a series of ten exhortations, as from a father to a son, that are designed to encourage the student to treasure and pursue the priceless gem of wisdom.

The benefits of wisdom are manifold, since they lead to true success and character in life as opposed to the pain and destruction that result from a life of folly. The discipline of wisdom leads to freedom and skillful living, whereas the path of foolishness and rebellion makes a person vulnerable to the lures and seductions of the lusts of this world. In this chapter, we are encouraged to diligently seek wisdom because of her many benefits.

READ PROVERBS 2

Prayer: *Lord, I want to treasure your words and incline my ear to wisdom. I know that you are the source of wisdom, and that you are a shield to those who fear you and walk in your ways.*

Meditation passage for today: verses 1-9

Day 158—Proverbs 3

The word translated "wisdom" (*hokhmah*) relates to the idea of skill. (It was used of Bezalel and Oholiab, the skillful men who fabricated the tabernacle.) This book stresses that it is through instruction, discipline, and practice that we learn the skill of living our lives in such a way that they produce what is excellent and worthwhile. When we fear the Lord by developing a sense of awe, humility, and dependence upon him, God refines us and shapes us into the people he wants us to become. God works on us as a skilled artist takes raw materials and transforms them into a beautiful work. Wisdom is derived from wholehearted trust in the Lord rather than ourselves. The opposite of wisdom is the folly of arrogance and autonomy.

READ PROVERBS 3

Prayer: *Lord, may I trust in you with all my heart and not lean on my own understanding. In all my ways I want to acknowledge you, so that you will make my paths straight.*

Meditation passage for today: verses 5–7

Day 159—Proverbs 4

The family was intended to be the relational context in which children are encouraged and instructed in the development of character, virtue, knowledge, and wisdom. One of the central messages in these nine chapters that introduce the maxims beginning in chapter 10 is that we can learn and live, not just live and learn. These are principles and precepts that have been hammered out long before us, and we do well to build upon this foundation of received knowledge and insight instead of reinventing the wheel ourselves. Each generation has the responsibility to impart these truths to the next.

READ PROVERBS 4

Prayer: *Lord, may I watch over my heart with all diligence, for from it flow the springs of life. May I put away from me a deceitful mouth and put devious speech far from me. May I look directly ahead and watch the path of my feet.*

Meditation passage for today: verses 7, 23–27

Day 160—Proverbs 5

The exhortations of Proverbs are both positive and negative, stressing both the benefits of wisdom and the destructive effects of foolishness. In this chapter, the son is warned about the subtle deceits of the immoral woman. These exhortations are preventive; they anticipate issues and temptations the child will face in the future. If we have not thought through our convictions in advance, they will not be there to serve us at the point of temptation. These verses counsel us to remain faithful to the spouse we have been given and warn us about the dangerous lures of infidelity and adultery.

READ PROVERBS 5

Prayer: *Lord, may I remember that my ways are ever before you and that you watch all my paths. Keep me from the snares of iniquity, and let me walk in fidelity to the relationships you have given me.*

Meditation passage for today: verses 1–2, 21

Day 161—Proverbs 6

Proverbs 6 is a collection of practical counsel in various areas of life. It warns us against financial commitments that can ensnare us down the road. It warns us about the trap of slothfulness and self-indulgence, and it counsels us to avoid those who stir up slander, strife, and discord among people. It also exhorts us to avoid the devastating consequences of immorality and adultery. All these instructions teach us to think before we act. Those who sin in haste will unfortunately have plenty of time for sorrow and repentance.

READ PROVERBS 6

Prayer: *Lord, may I carefully listen to these words of strong counsel concerning money, sloth, self-indulgence, slander, discord, pride, deceitfulness, and immorality.*

Meditation passage for today: verses 20–23

Day 162—Proverbs 7

Proverbs 7 and 8 contrast folly and wisdom by personifying them as two radically different women. The woman of folly is portrayed as a seductress who flatters the naïve with her words and who presents herself not only in open places but also in dark corners. She can be subtle and persuasive, and she seduces by appeals to pride and rationalization. Her speech is enticing and persistent. Those who are lured into the trap of folly never think about the disastrous consequences of the way that leads to death.

READ PROVERBS 7

Prayer: *Lord, may I keep your words and treasure your commands within me. Help me not to be tempted by the lures and entrapments of the way of folly. May I remember that yielding to the seductions of money, sex, and power draw me away from you.*

Meditation passage for today: verses 1–5

Day 163—Proverbs 8

The beautiful personification of wisdom as a woman in chapter 8 is a portrait of the perfection of righteousness and morality (verses 8-9). This wisdom is divine (verses 22-31) and is the wellspring of all biological and spiritual life (3:18; 8:35-36). Proverbs stresses that wisdom is not limited to an elite class of people but is accessible to all who are willing to seek it. As the New Testament teaches, Christ Jesus is the incarnation of wisdom: He "became to us wisdom from God, and righteousness and sanctification, and redemption" (1 Cor 1:30). In Christ "are hidden all the treasures of wisdom and knowledge" (Col 2:3).

READ PROVERBS 8

Prayer: *Lord, may I listen to your instruction and be wise enough to respond to your exhortations. In your favor I find life. Let me love you and your ways, and thus avoid the ways of death.*

Meditation passage for today: verses 32-36

Day 164—Proverbs 9

The proverbs themselves do not begin until chapter 10, and in this last preparatory chapter, wisdom is personified as a virtuous woman who invites those who lack understanding to come to her well-provisioned table.

These pithy sayings of Solomon and others cover a wide variety of issues, though for the most part, they are not arranged in any topical manner. The Hebrew word *mashal,* "proverb," means a comparison or a similitude, and the proverbs use figures of speech to make comparisons and penetrating insights. The proverbs, based upon careful observations of accumulated experience, were designed to be easily committed to memory, and they are simple illustrations that expose fundamental realities about life.

READ PROVERBS 9

Prayer: *Lord, thank you for your gracious invitation to receive the abundance of life and blessings you offer. May the Book of Proverbs teach me that the fear of the Lord is the beginning of wisdom, and the knowledge of the Holy One is understanding.*

Meditation passage for today: verse 10

Day 165—Proverbs 31

Proverbs concludes with a number of precepts and comparisons by Agur (chapter 30) and Lemuel (chapter 31). Chapter 31 ends with an acrostic (the first letter of each verse consecutively moves through the alphabet of twenty-two Hebrew letters) depicting a wife of noble character (verses 10–31). This timeless portrait of a wise woman is an ever-relevant model for women. She is intelligent, creative, industrious, prudent, and discerning. She plans carefully and makes informed decisions that benefit others. She manages her household with diligence and grace, and she looks to the Lord as her source of strength.

READ PROVERBS 31

Prayer: *Lord, thank you for this portrait of the woman of virtue, dignity, diligence, and grace. I thank you that in every time and culture, these principles can be applied by those who seek you first.*

Meditation passage for today: verses 30–31

Day 166—Ecclesiastes 3

The need for satisfaction and significance in life drives most people to pursue these things in the wrong places. We pursue the created order rather than the Creator of order. Ecclesiastes, written by a king (evidently Solomon) whose abilities, assets, and attainments are far beyond our own, serves as a road map that shows us where the human quest apart from God ends up. It is a warning, by a person who had it all, that the world will never satisfy our deepest longings. These can only be satisfied in a relationship with the living God. This is because we have been created in his image, and thus he has "set eternity in [our] heart" (3:11).

READ ECCLESIASTES 3

Prayer: *Lord, you have made everything appropriate in its appointed time. You have set eternity in our hearts, yet no one can discern the whole of your plan. Thank you that whatever you do endures.*

Meditation passage for today: verses 1, 11

Day 167—Ecclesiastes 12

Ecclesiastes was written at the end of an unprecedented pursuit of wisdom, power, pleasure, possessions, and accomplishments. It uses this experience to demonstrate that none of these things can fill the empty void in the human heart. Augustine said that God created us for himself, and our hearts are restless until they find their rest in him.

Ecclesiastes is a commentary on this truth: The search for the highest good must not be limited to that which is "under the sun" (this expression appears twenty-nine times) but must end in the fear and obedience of God (12:13).

READ ECCLESIASTES 12

Prayer: *Lord, I know that apart from you, life is empty, meaningless, and futile. It is characterized by inequity, injustice, and uncertainty. With you there is hope, meaning, and reason for rejoicing.*

Meditation passage for today: verses 1, 13–14

Day 168—Song of Solomon 1

This beautiful homage to the love that germinates and blossoms between a man and a woman stood out among the 1,005 songs written by Solomon (see 1 Kgs 4:32) as "the Song of Songs." It is a literary masterpiece of Oriental symbolism, layered metaphors, and rich imagery that eulogizes the glories of romantic love. This song is intimate, yet it never sinks to vulgarity in its portrayal of attraction, desire, pleasure, consummation, separation, companionship, and growth in the relationship between lovers. The physical and emotional aspects of marital love are a gift from God, and they are designed to be enjoyed in an other-centered way.

READ SONG OF SOLOMON 1

Prayer: *Lord, this poetic portrait of love between a man and a woman also points to the intimate relationship you invite us to have with you. I ask for the grace of increased passion for you.*

Meditation passage for today: verse 4

Day 169—Isaiah 6

Isaiah has been called "the Shakespeare of the prophets" and "the Mount Everest of Hebrew prophecy" for good reasons. This comprehensive and superbly written book is the high water mark of messianic prophecy, and it can be regarded as the Bible in miniature. The first thirty-nine chapters loosely correspond to the thirty-nine books of the Old Testament in their condemnation of sin and emphasis on judgment. The last twenty-seven chapters loosely correspond to the twenty-seven books of the New Testament in their message of consolation and hope.

Chapter 6 presents a vision of the majesty of the living God and the commissioning of Isaiah to a prophetic mission to God's rebellious people.

READ ISAIAH 6

Prayer: *Lord, you are awesome in holiness, and the whole earth is full of your glory. I thank you that you are concerned for the welfare of your people and that you want us to find life, blessing, and hope in you.*

Meditation passage for today: verses 1–5

Day 170—Isaiah 40

This beautiful chapter dramatically introduces the prophecies of comfort that conclude the Book of Isaiah. It is with sorrow that Isaiah announces in the first thirty–nine chapters that the kingdom of Judah will go into captivity because of her continual rebellion against the Lord. However, chapters 40–66 proclaim a glorious message of future hope and blessings for the people of God.

Isaiah 40 opens with a word of comfort and anticipation of God's personal deliverance and grace for those who look to him. With magnificent poetic imagery, the wisdom, sovereignty, majesty, and the perfect ways of God are unfolded.

READ ISAIAH 40

Prayer: *Lord, thank you for your lovingkindness, your infinite wisdom, your limitless power, your wonderful beauty, and your authority over all things. I take comfort in your changeless character, and I wait upon you alone.*

Meditation passage for today: verses 11, 25–26, 31

Day 171—Isaiah 53

Isaiah is the most comprehensive of the Old Testament prophets and offers the clearest portrait of the coming Messiah. Isaiah has rightly been called the "Saint Paul of the Old Testament" because of his systematic exposition, his clarity and power, his sweeping scope, and his striking imagery. He is quoted in the New Testament more than any other prophet, with about eighty-five allusions to chapter 53 alone.

This text presents five aspects of the saving work of the Messiah: (1) his sacrifice was wholehearted (burnt offering; 52:13–15), (2) his character was perfect (meal offering; 53:1–3), (3) he brought atonement that issues in peace with God (peace offering; 53:4–6), (4) he paid for the transgression of the people (sin offering; 53:7–9), and (5) he died for the effects of sin (trespass offering; 53:10–12).

READ ISAIAH 53

Prayer: *Lord, thanks for this clear portrait of the saving work of Christ that was written seven centuries before his crucifixion. Thank you that he suffered sinlessly, silently, and as a substitute for us.*

Meditation passage for today: verses 3–7, 12

Day 172—Isaiah 55

The prophetic condemnation (chapters 1–39) is followed by a prophetic consolation (chapters 40–66) in which the Lord comforts his people with a message of hope and restoration. The sovereignty and majesty of God was the foundation for Israel's hope (chapters 40–48). He alone rules the realms of nature and nations, and his power and greatness is contrasted with the impotence of idols. The salvation of God centered on the redemptive work of the coming Servant who would save his people from their iniquities (49–57).

In this chapter, the Messiah invites everyone to come and find life in him. Those who seek the Lord will be satisfied with his righteousness.

READ ISAIAH 55

Prayer: *Lord, I will seek you while you may be found, and call upon you while you are near. I forsake evil and return to you, and I thank you that you have compassion on me and abundantly pardon.*

Meditation passage for today: verses 1, 6–11

Day 173—Isaiah 61

In chapters 58–66, the restoration of God will extend to all who have come to him in humility and trust. Messiah himself will reign over the earth in his glorious kingdom.

Jesus the Messiah quoted verses 1–2a in the synagogue in Nazareth (see Lk 4:18–19) and told his hearers that these words were fulfilled in him. It is significant that he stopped before the words "and the day of vengeance of our God," since this concerns his second advent. The Lord loves justice and will bring an everlasting kingdom of righteousness, rejoicing, and praise upon the earth.

READ ISAIAH 61

Prayer: *Lord, I will rejoice greatly in you, and my soul will exult in my God. For you have clothed me with garments of salvation and have wrapped me with a robe of righteousness.*

Meditation passage for today: verses 1–2, 8, 10

Day 174—Jeremiah 18

Jeremiah was called to the unenviable prophetic ministry of urging a rebellious people to repentance for nearly five decades without any significant positive response. Instead, he experienced public humiliation, was put in stocks, was forced to flee for his life, was thrown into a cistern, and was misunderstood by virtually all who encountered him. In spite of his frequent discouragement and pain, he remained faithful to his calling and endured to the end. He is a striking model of faithfulness and steadfast endurance in the face of opposition.

The sign of the potter in Jeremiah 18 is an object lesson that illustrates the opportunity God gives his people to repent before they are judged, and their stubborn refusal to do so.

READ JEREMIAH 18

Prayer: *Lord, I do not want to walk according to my own plans or follow the vain imaginations of my heart. May I be responsive to your call and return to you when I stray from your ways.*

Meditation passage for today: verses 6, 11–12

Day 175—Jeremiah 19

The sign of the potter's earthenware jar is another illustration to the people of Judah of the irrevocable consequences of their apostasy, idolatry, and immorality.

Jeremiah took some of the elders of the people and priests to the Valley of Hinnom, near the potsherd gate of Jerusalem, and proclaimed a prophetic word of condemnation due to the spiritual infidelity of the people. Then Jeremiah shattered the jar in their sight to portray the way God would break the people and the city. This scene summarizes the prophetic burden of this whole book: In spite of God's covenant love for his people, they have corrupted themselves through spiritual harlotry and are beyond the point of repentance.

READ JEREMIAH 19

Prayer: *Lord, your character is perfect and uncompromisingly holy. My own thoughts, words, and deeds have separated me from you. Thank you for restoring my peace and union with you through the gift of faith in the righteousness of Christ.*

Meditation passage for today: verse 15

Day 176—Jeremiah 31

Jeremiah's prophecy about the coming new covenant anticipates the new covenant that was inaugurated through the
blood of Christ (see Mt 26:26–29). In spite of the prophetic
condemnation of Judah because of the people's sin and
rebellion, there is also a prophetic consolation because of
God's mercy and grace.

In verses 31–34, the Lord proclaims that he will make a
new covenant with Israel and Judah in which he will implant
his righteousness in their hearts and take away their iniquity.
Unlike the Mosaic covenant, which was external and could
not be fulfilled by human effort or merit, the new covenant
is internal and is fulfilled by God's indwelling Spirit.

READ JEREMIAH 31

Prayer: *Lord, you inaugurated the new covenant through the blood of
your Son. Thank you that you have made me a beneficiary of this
covenant through faith in his completed work. Thank you that Christ
now dwells in me, and I in him.*

Meditation passage for today: verses 3, 31–34

Day 177—Lamentations 3

The sad and mournful set of five elegiac poems known as Lamentations is striking in its emotional content, its beauty, and its literary structure. Writing with a broken heart, Jeremiah identifies with the sorrow of his people and the apparent destruction of their future, but he pauses to remember the faithfulness and lovingkindness of his God. It is a reminder to us to hold fast to God's character, especially in the distressing times of life.

In the third lament, Jeremiah empathizes with the anguish and despondency of his people but also finds hope when he considers the compassion and faithfulness of the Lord.

READ LAMENTATIONS 3

Prayer: *Lord, may I call to mind that your lovingkindness indeed never ceases. Your compassions never fail. They are new every morning; great is your faithfulness. "The Lord is my portion," says my soul, "therefore I have hope in him."*

Meditation passage for today: verses 22–26

Day 178—Ezekiel 1

Ezekiel is an extraordinary book of mystery, visions, symbolism, parables, and allegories that expands our thinking about the glory and majestic splendor of God. The book invites us to fear him and hope in him. This is a complex and multifaceted collection of prophetic oracles, and it offers a number of significant keys to grasping God's future plan to bring salvation and righteousness to the earth.

Ezekiel's vision of the glory of God in chapter 1 is one of the most remarkable passages in Scripture. It is the first of a series of passages that trace the localized manifestation of the presence of God's glory from its departure from the temple to its return to the new temple (1:28; 3:12, 23; 9:3; 10:4, 18–19; 11:22–23; 43:1–5; 44:4).

READ EZEKIEL 1

Prayer: *Lord, I marvel at your awesome being, majesty, and holiness. Your Word revealing the appearance of the likeness of your glory transcends my comprehension. I realize how little I really know about you.*

Meditation passage for today: verses 4, 22, 26–28

Day 179—Ezekiel 37

After Ezekiel was divinely commissioned to be a prophet to the Jewish exiles in Babylon (chapters 2–3), he delivered a series of prophetic condemnations that focused first on Judah (chapters 4–24) and then on the surrounding nations (chapters 25–32). The final section of Ezekiel's prophecy (chapters 33–48) was delivered after Jerusalem's destruction. It turns from the theme of condemnation to a message of consolation.

God's judgment came just as he promised; his promise of the future blessing, gathering, and restoration of Israel will just as surely be fulfilled. The dramatic vision of the reanimation of the dry bones anticipates the restoration and purification of Israel and Judah. The book concludes with details of the new temple, the new Jerusalem, and the new land (chapters 40–48).

READ EZEKIEL 37

Prayer: *Lord, thank you that you are faithful to your covenant promises in spite of the unfaithfulness of your people. I am grateful for this vision of restoration, renewal, and the reign of the coming King.*

Meditation passage for today: verses 3–6, 12–14, 26–28

Day 180—Daniel 1

Daniel is an extraordinary book; it contains a sweeping overview of the rise and fall of the kingdoms of men, the anticipation of the kingdom ruled by the Messiah that will never fall, and a fascinating portrait of the prophet himself. Daniel's remarkable life from his teenage years to the time of his old age illustrates a variety of biblical principles that are relevant to our lives as people who live in a culture that is hostile to spiritual growth and commitment.

Daniel's personal background and preparation is presented in chapter 1. Daniel and his friends remained faithful to the Lord and refused to compromise their convictions during the time of their training for service in Babylon.

READ DANIEL 1

Prayer: *Lord, the example of this faithful and godly figure challenges me to honor you and avoid areas of compromise in my life. May I walk before you in dependence upon the indwelling righteousness of Christ.*

Meditation passage for today: verses 8–9

Day 181—Daniel 2

In chapters 2–7, the language switches from Hebrew to Aramaic, since this portion of the book outlines God's sovereign plan for the Gentiles. The visions and interpretations in this section reveal how God would raise up and overthrow four Gentile empires, after which he was to establish an everlasting kingdom.

The dream of Nebuchadnezzar in chapter 2 illustrates the primary theme of this book—the power and dominion of God over human affairs. The God of Israel has authority over all nations. It is he who changes the times and the epochs; he removes kings and establishes kings; he gives wisdom to wise men and knowledge to men of understanding (2:20–22).

READ DANIEL 2

Prayer: *Lord, you have authority over all history and over all the kingdoms of this world. I am grateful for the sure hope that these temporal kingdoms will be replaced by your everlasting kingdom through the sovereign reign of the Lord Jesus.*

Meditation passage for today: verses 20–22

Day 182—Daniel 3

Seeing himself as the head of gold in his dream in Daniel 2, Nebuchadnezzar erected a golden image and demanded that all bow to it. Daniel's three friends, who had been appointed to positions of authority, were accused by their enemies of disloyalty to the king because of their refusal to worship this image. When they respectfully declined the king's urging to bow to the image, Nebuchadnezzar was furious and ordered that they be burned alive in a superheated furnace. The king was stunned to see them walking unharmed in the fire, accompanied by an awesome being. The persecution and preservation of Daniel's friends illustrates the power of God to protect his people in times of tribulation.

READ DANIEL 3

Prayer: *Lord, help me follow the example of these men who trusted you regardless of the outcome. Help me depend completely on your character both in smooth and in troubled times. May I honor you by putting no conditions on my trust.*

Meditation passage for today: verses 17–18, 28

Day 183—Daniel 4

N ebuchadnezzar was alarmed by a night vision of a great tree that was reduced to a stump. He called Daniel to interpret the dream when his diviners could not. Daniel was appalled by the meaning of the vision but faithfully related it to the king, urging him to avert the disaster by turning from his iniquities and showing mercy to the poor.

The king was too proud to heed this wise counsel, and the Lord fulfilled the vision by reducing him to an animal–like state for seven years. At the end of this time, the Lord restored Nebuchadnezzar's reason and reestablished his kingdom. The now humbled king gave honor to the Most High God, "who does according to his will in the host of heaven and among the inhabitants of earth."

READ DANIEL 4

Prayer: *Lord, I know that you, the Most High, are ruler over the realm of mankind, and that you bestow authority on whom you wish. Deliver me from the folly of pride when circumstances appear to go my way, and let me walk in wisdom, fearing your holy name.*

Meditation passage for today: verses 17, 25, 34–35

Day 184—Daniel 5

After his long reign over Babylon (605–562 B.C.), Nebuchadnezzar was succeeded by three kings with brief reigns, and then by his son-in-law Nabonidus (556–539 B.C.). Since he was constantly fighting the Medes and Persians, Nabonidus arranged a coregency with his son Belshazzar (553–539 B.C.). In his last feast, Belshazzar defied the God of Israel by using gold vessels from the former temple in Jerusalem.

When a hand appeared and wrote on the palace wall, the terrified king sought an interpreter. Daniel was summoned out of obscurity. The prophet rebuked the king for his pride and predicted the overthrow of Babylon in his interpretation of the writing. That night the Persians diverted the water of the Euphrates, went under the gates, and took over the city.

READ DANIEL 5

Prayer: *Lord, those who exalt themselves against the Lord of heaven will be cast down. May I humble myself before you and glorify your name and not my own.*

Meditation passage for today: verses 21–23

Day 185—Daniel 6

During the reign of Darius the Mede, Daniel so distinguished himself that the commissioners and satraps saw him as a threat. To overthrow Daniel, they manipulated Darius to sign a document forbidding people to make petitions to anyone but him for thirty days, on pain of death. Knowing Daniel's habit of praying three times a day, they accused him of violating the injunction. Darius was trapped by his own edict and forced to condemn Daniel to the lions' den. The next morning, the king was delighted to find that God had delivered Daniel. He issued a decree honoring the God of Daniel.

READ DANIEL 6

Prayer: *Lord, thank you for the character, conviction, and faithfulness of your servant Daniel. May I never lose sight of your sovereignty, and may I walk steadily with you in spite of fluctuating circumstances. May I walk so closely to you during my lifetime that my actions demand an explanation from those who do not know you.*

Meditation passage for today: verses 5, 16, 22–23

Day 186—Daniel 9

In chapters 8–12, the language switches from Aramaic back to Hebrew, since this section overviews God's prophetic plan for Israel. These chapters describe Israel under the Medo–Persian and Grecian empires and detail the coming kings of Persia and Greece. The wars between the Ptolemies of Egypt and the Seleucids of Syria and the persecution under Antiochus Epiphanes in the second century B.C. are also described. The people of God would be delivered from tribulation and raised from the dead (chapter 12).

Chapter 9 records the third of Daniel's four visions. After his prayer of confession on behalf of his people, God's faithful servant was given the revelation of the seventy weeks, which gave God's plan for the redemption and deliverance of his people and predicted the time of the Messiah's atoning death.

READ DANIEL 9

Prayer: *Lord, your Word clarifies my present experience by giving me perspective on your plan and purposes. You are the great and awesome God, who keeps your covenant and lovingkindness for those who love you and keep your commandments.*

Meditation passage for today: verses 4–5, 24–27

Day 187—Hosea 4

Hosea ("salvation") was a prophet to the northern kingdom of Israel (often named Ephraim after its largest tribe; 5:3–13) in the days of its last six kings. Hosea's lengthy time of service (from about 755 B.C. to about 710 B.C.) made him a contemporary of Isaiah and Micah and a younger contemporary of Amos, who also prophesied to the northern kingdom.

Hosea's personal affliction (chapters 1–3) illustrated Israel's coming national catastrophe (chapters 4–14). After bearing him three children, Gomer abandoned Hosea and became an adulteress. When she was reduced to slavery, Hosea publicly redeemed her and restored her. In the same way, Israel committed spiritual adultery through corruption, injustice, and willful idolatry, and she resolutely refused to repent (chapters 4–7).

READ HOSEA 4

Prayer: *Lord, may I never succumb to pride by taking your gifts and benefits for granted. When I sin against you, give me a humble willingness to repent and yield the control of my life to you.*

Meditation passage for today: verses 1, 6, 10

Day 188—Hosea 14

Due to Israel's hardness of heart, she would be brought into a judgment of dispersion and destruction (chapters 8–10). God's holiness and justice required him to discipline Israel, but because of his steadfast love and compassion, he would restore Israel in the future (chapters 11–14).

The book of Hosea offers a profound illustration of the way we are loved by God. His love for us is unconditional, but it is also marked by his holiness. God seeks better things for us than the things we choose for ourselves. This book reminds us of our need to turn back to the Lover of our souls whenever we have strayed from him.

READ HOSEA 14

Prayer: *Lord, I know that your ways are right. Help me to be righteous so that I will walk in your ways. I thank you that when I stumble, I can return to you and receive your cleansing grace.*

Meditation passage for today: verses 1–2, 4, 9

Day 189—Joel 2

Joel's theme is the Day of the Lord that will come upon Judah and the nations. He used Judah's dreadful experience of a recent locust plague to illustrate the devastation that awaited the nation if they did not humbly turn to the Lord in repentance and obedience. The Lord appealed through his prophet to "return to me with all your heart, and with fasting, weeping and mourning" (2:12). Images of disaster are prominent in this book, including not only locust plagues but also famine, fires, invading armies, and phenomena in the heavens. After their judgment was completed, the people of Judah and all who call on the name of the Lord would be saved (2:32).

READ JOEL 2

Prayer: *Lord, when I stray, may I always return to you, for you are gracious and compassionate, slow to anger and abounding in lovingkindness.*

Meditation passage for today: verses 12–13, 25, 27–32

Day 190—Amos 1

Although Amos lived in Judah (Tekoa was twelve miles south of Jerusalem), he was sent by God as a prophet to the northern kingdom of Israel. "I am not a prophet, nor am I the son of a prophet; for I am a herdsman and grower of sycamore figs. But the Lord took me from following the flock and the Lord said to me, 'Go, prophesy to my people Israel'" (7:14–15).

Amos, like James in the New Testament, did not mince words but delivered a series of sharp and incisive declarations and images that aroused the conscience and required a response. This book is relevant to our times because it was addressed to a materialistic culture that fostered greed, injustice, and arrogance. It is a word of warning that such a culture cannot continue for long without being diminished by divine judgment.

READ AMOS 1

Prayer: *Lord, you are an awesome and holy God, and I must order my steps before you in repentance and righteousness. May I make a difference in my time by expressing your righteousness in the way I live and relate to others.*

Meditation passage for today: verse 2

Day 191—Amos 2

The Book of Amos begins with a series of eight prophetic oracles that pronounce judgment on the nations that surround Israel (chapters 1–2). The word *fire*, a symbol of judgment, often appears in this section, and as a map will show, the sequence of the seven nations gradually spirals in on the last nation, Israel. This "funnel of fire" demonstrates the iniquities of these countries, and that judgment is unavoidable. In three sermons, each beginning with the phrase, "Hear this word" (3:1; 4:1; 5:1), Amos outlines the reasons for Israel's coming overthrow. In spite of all that God has done, he tells them, "yet you have not returned to me" (4:6, 8–11). Due to their refusal to turn to him, he would send them into exile beyond Damascus (5:27).

READ AMOS 2

Prayer: *Lord, may I listen responsively to your Word with a heart to obey your exhortations and walk in your truth.*

Meditation passage for today: verses 4, 6

Day 192—Amos 9

In a series of five visions (7:1–9:10), Amos pictured the coming judgment on the northern kingdom of Israel. Due to Amos' intercession, the first two judgments of locusts and fire would not take place. In the vision of the plumb line, Israel was like a leaning wall; in the vision of the basket of ripe fruit, Israel was rotten and overripe for judgment.

Amos was an extraordinarily concise and penetrating prophet who multiplied oracles and images to hammer home the solemn theme of inescapable judgment. Only in the last five verses is there a message of hope and promise. The three promises at the end of the book (9:11–15) are that God will restore the line of David, rebuild the nation, and renew the people.

READ AMOS 9

Prayer: *Lord, you are faithful to keep your promises in spite of our unfaithfulness. May I order my steps before you and walk in hope.*

Meditation passage for today: verses 5–6, 13–15

Day 193—Obadiah

With only twenty-one verses, Obadiah is the shortest book in the Old Testament, and yet it is a complete message with the twin prophetic themes of condemnation (verses 1–16) and consolation (verses 17–21). The consolation portion concerns Judah, not Edom. The burden of Obadiah is a pronouncement of inescapable doom upon the Edomites (Esau) because they looked down on their brother Judah (Jacob) in the day of his misfortune and rejoiced over the people of Judah in the day of their disaster (verses 12–14). The Edomites' pride would be brought low (verses 3–4), and they would be ransacked (verse 6), terrified (verse 9), and obliterated (verse 10). Israel, on the other hand, would be restored, and it would possess its inheritance (verses 17–21).

READ OBADIAH

Prayer: *Lord, I realize that the things we do to other people may eventually haunt us. We can either sow to please the flesh and reap corruption, or we can sow to please the Spirit and reap blessing.*

Meditation passage for today: verses 3–4, 15, 17

Day 194—Jonah 1

Everything in Jonah (the storm, the lots, the sailors, the great fish, the people of Nineveh, the vine, the worm, and the east wind) obeyed God's commands except for the prophet himself. God told Jonah to go northeast to Nineveh; instead, he got on a boat that was heading west to Tarshish (possibly Spain). He knew that if he preached a message of repentance to the Assyrians, they might respond, and this would make him feel like a traitor to his own people. God's purpose would not be thwarted, however, and he sovereignly prepared a great fish to deliver the disobedient prophet and to change his perspective.

READ JONAH 1

Prayer: *Lord, disobedience to your calling creates pain and confusion in my life. Thank you that my failures do not disqualify me from your service. When I fail, help me to be willing to repent and return to you.*

Meditation passage for today: verses 9, 16–17

Day 195—Jonah 2

Jonah's prayer of praise to God for delivering him from a watery grave was followed by a divine recommissioning to preach to the people of Nineveh. God prepared a "great fish" (the text does not say "whale") to preserve Jonah and deliver him on dry land. The fish and its divinely appointed rendezvous with the sinking prophet became a powerful reminder to Jonah of the sovereignty of God in every circumstance.

Jonah's experience of being engulfed by the deep, engorged by a great fish, and later deposited alive on land was used by Christ as a type of his death, burial, and resurrection (see Mt 12:39–40).

READ JONAH 2

Prayer: *Lord, thank you that you care for and discipline us as your children. Thank you as well for all the ways you deliver us. I affirm that salvation is from the Lord.*

Meditation passage for today: verses 7, 9

Day 196—Jonah 3

Jonah obeyed God's second commission to go to Nineveh, where he became "a sign to the Ninevites" (Lk 11:30). (The prophet would have been a walking object lesson from God if his skin was bleached from hours in the stomach of the fish.) As he moved through the city, his one–sentence sermon evoked a remarkable response of repentance and fasting among the people of Nineveh. Due to his great mercy, God "relented concerning the calamity which he had declared he would bring upon them."

Thus, Jesus declared, "The men of Nineveh will stand up with this generation at the judgment, and will condemn it because they repented at the preaching of Jonah; and behold, something greater than Jonah is here" (Mt 12:41).

READ JONAH 3

Prayer: *Lord, I am grateful that you are gracious and compassionate, slow to anger and abundant in lovingkindness, and one who relents concerning calamity.*

Meditation passage for today: verses 9–10

Day 197—Jonah 4

When the Ninevites responded with repentance and fasting, Jonah reacted with anger rather than rejoicing. He resented God's willingness to show mercy to his enemies. The Lord taught Jonah a lesson on compassion by using a vine as an object lesson.

We typically want God to treat us with grace and to treat our enemies with justice. Jonah is the story of a man who resisted God's call to prophesy to the capital city of Israel's archenemy, Assyria. He was afraid that if he prophesied to the people of Nineveh, they would repent and God would avert the disaster that was due to come in forty days. This little book teaches us about the folly of resenting the grace of God when it is extended to people we think should not receive it. We can be thankful that God's mercy moves beyond national borders.

READ JONAH 4

Prayer: *Lord, your intentions extend beyond our personal needs and desires, since you are the ruler not only of nature but also of all nations. May I never allow my personal bias to stand between me and your purposes.*

Meditation passage for today: verses 2, 10–11

Day 198—Micah 5

The prophecy of Micah opens with a declaration of coming judgment upon the northern kingdom of Israel (Samaria) and the southern kingdom of Judah (Jerusalem). The cause of this judgment was listed as premeditated crime, covetousness, fraud, and lying prophets (1:1–2:11). Nevertheless, there is a word of hope in God's promises of regathering and deliverance (2:12–13).

Micah focused his prophetic barbs on the ungodly rulers and false prophets of Israel and Judah, and he predicted a disaster coming upon them (verse 3). This word of condemnation is followed by a consoling announcement of future restoration through the reinstitution of the kingdom under the rule of the Messiah (verses 4–5).

READ MICAH 5

Prayer: *Lord, I am grateful for your promise that you will do what people in all ages have failed to do—bring in a kingdom of universal peace, justice, and righteousness.*

Meditation passage for today: verses 2, 4

Day 199—Micah 7

In the concluding section of this book (chapters 6–7), God called the people into court and summoned the whole earth to witness against them (6:1–2; see also 1:2). In spite of God's acts of gracious deliverance, his people had rejected him and walked in dishonesty, injustice, and treachery. But the book closes with a series of promises that God would restore the remnant and pardon their transgressions (7:7–20).

Micah's particular concern was with the social sins of exploitation and injustice. There were many problems in Israel and Judah: political corruption, greed and arrogance among religious leaders, and false prophets who were more interested in personal gain than in corporate goodness. As the prophet of the poor and the downtrodden, Micah has particular relevance to the conditions we face in our own culture.

READ MICAH 7

Prayer: Lord, may I do justice, love kindness, and walk humbly before you. You are the God who pardons iniquity and delights in unchanging love.

Meditation passage for today: verses 7, 18–20

Day 200—Nahum 1

Nahum's prophecy opens with a description of Yahweh's righteous character. He is "a jealous and avenging God" who "takes vengeance on his adversaries" (1:2). His power is unlimited, and no one can endure his anger (1:3–6). Those who trust in him discover his goodness and grace, but he overcomes his foes (1:7–8). Since he is holy, he condemned the wickedness of Nineveh (1:9–14) and comforted those who were righteous in Judah (1:15).

Using vivid imagery, Nahum described the siege and the plundering of Nineveh after the invading warriors moved through the breach in its wall (chapter 2). As the chariots and charging cavalry invaded, the city was thrown into chaos and there was no one to mourn for it (3:1–7). Just as the Assyrians overthrew Thebes, Egypt's proud capital, so Assyria's capital also would be destroyed in spite of its many fortifications (3:8–18). Due to Assyria's cruelty, everyone would rejoice at its fall (3:19).

READ NAHUM 1

Prayer: *Lord, you are good, a stronghold in the day of trouble, and you know those who take refuge in you. May I never presume on your grace but trust wholly in you.*

Meditation passage for today: verses 2–3, 7, 15

Day 201—Habakkuk 3

When Habakkuk saw the growing wickedness in his countrymen as they shamelessly disobeyed the laws of God and openly distorted justice on every level, he wondered how God could allow this to go on without bringing Judah to judgment. God's answer to his question was that he was raising up the Babylonians as his rod of judgment on Judah. This answer only increased Habakkuk's confusion. The Babylonians were even more violent and depraved than the people of Judah—how could God allow this? God's second answer helped him better understand the goodness, perfection, wisdom, and power of Yahweh. With a clearer grasp of the *Person* of the Lord, he had a greater capacity to trust the *purposes* of the Lord. Thus, Habakkuk could conclude his book with confidence rather than complaint, and with praise rather than perplexity.

READ HABAKKUK 3

Prayer: *Lord, teach me to live by faith and by hope in you, especially in times when the circumstances surrounding me make me question whether you are in control and know what you are doing.*

Meditation passage for today: verses 17–19

Day 202—Zephaniah 3

Like the majority of Old Testament prophets, Zephaniah developed the twin themes of condemnation (1:1–3:8) and consolation (3:9–20). The bulk of the book concerns the primary theme of judgment, and like Joel before him, Zephaniah's central image of judgment is "the Day of the Lord." This image appears twenty-three times in different forms in this short book of three chapters, and it refers to a judgment that was universal (1:2–3; 3:8), imminent (1:14), and wrathful (1:15–17). Yet there is another side of the Day of the Lord that pointed to restoration (3:9–13) and blessing (3:14–20).

Zephaniah is a powerful and condensed book that uses vivid and gripping imagery to communicate an unrelenting message about the day of judgment. This day would come not only to Judah and the nations that surrounded Judah, but it also will come in the future to all the nations of the earth.

READ ZEPHANIAH 3

Prayer: *Lord, I thank you that you exult over your loved ones with joy, that you are quiet in your love, and that you rejoice over your people with shouts of joy.*

Meditation passage for today: verses 5, 9, 15, 17

Day 203—Haggai 1

This brief prophecy was delivered to a people whose spiritual lives were in decline because they had allowed their priorities to become misplaced. In a series of sharp exhortations, Haggai encouraged them to consider their ways, to take action, and to take heart. This little book provides a strong word to us when we find ourselves discouraged and despondent because of spiritual lethargy.

In his first sermon to the Jewish remnant, Haggai told them that they needed to reorder their priorities. They were more concerned with their own comfort than with their spiritual well-being, and as a consequence, God was withholding his material blessing. Zerubbabel, the governor of Judah; Joshua the high priest; and the whole remnant responded to Haggai's message, and they resumed construction on the temple (1:1–15).

READ HAGGAI 1

Prayer: *Lord, I thank you that when we value the spiritual above the material in our lives, you take care of our material needs. Help me remember that when we value the material above the spiritual, we not only miss out on the spiritual but are never satisfied with the material.*

Meditation passage for today: verses 12–13

Day 204—Haggai 2

Haggai's second sermon was a word of encouragement that in spite of the small scale of the second temple, its glory would be greater than that of the former temple, and it would be a place of peace (2:1–9). The third message of this book was addressed to the priests and concerned purification from the contamination of sin and the need for obedience (2:10–19). The final oracle reaffirmed God's plan to overthrow the nations of the earth (2:20–23; cf. 2:6–7).

Haggai called the Jewish remnant to the realization that God actually increased their hardships to get their attention. Those hardships caused them to look to him, rather than to themselves, to meet their needs. If they would seek him first and honor him by finishing the temple, God would bless them and provide for their material needs.

READ HAGGAI 2

Prayer: *Lord, may I look to you and not my work as the source of my provision. I know that you use my work as a means, but you are the source. When I forget this, I confess I put my security in money by planning according to income rather than according to priorities. Help me align my values with your kingdom.*

Meditation passage for today: verses 4–9

Day 205—Zechariah 14

The visions and exhortations of Zechariah 1–8 were given to the prophet in Jerusalem during the rebuilding of the temple by the returned remnant. The purpose of this portion of the book (dated from November of 520 B.C. to December of 518 B.C.) was to encourage the people to complete the new central sanctuary and to help them realize that it was not simply a building but a key to their spiritual identity. The Messiah would appear in this very temple when he came to bring salvation to his people.

Zechariah evidently received the two oracles of chapters 9–14 a few decades after the completion of the temple in 516 B.C., and they are directly concerned with the coming Messiah and Israel's restoration after the time of the Gentiles. These oracles were given to comfort and reassure the remnant that despite the uncertainties and hardships they were encountering, the Lord regathered them for a purpose. He had a glorious future for them in the messianic kingdom.

READ ZECHARIAH 14

Prayer: *Lord, I am grateful for this promise of the Messiah's coming to be King over all the earth. Come quickly, Lord Jesus!*

Meditation passage for today: verses 3–5, 9

Day 206—Malachi 3

Malachi delivered this oracle as a dialogue between God and his people. The Lord sought to penetrate the barriers that the priests and people had erected between themselves and their God. The religious and moral corruption of the people reveal a condition of spiritual lethargy marked by an attitude that it did not pay to serve the Lord. They had convinced themselves that in spite of their religious observances, God had not alleviated their difficult circumstances. But the Lord told them that their lack of blessing was not due to divine indifference but to their hypocrisy, lack of sincerity, and disobedience to his moral law. When they repented and returned to God, God would return to them (3:7) and bless their labors.

READ MALACHI 3

Prayer: *Lord, when my religious observances become stale and meaningless, help me renew a wholehearted desire to honor and trust you.*

Meditation passage for today: verses 1–3, 6–7

Day 207—Malachi 4

Malachi anticipated the coming of the Lord's messenger who would prepare the way for the Messiah. "Behold, I am going to send my messenger, and he will clear the way before me.... Behold, I am going to send you Elijah the prophet before the coming of the great and terrible day of the Lord" (3:1; 4:5; see Is 40:3).

One aspect of this was fulfilled by John the Baptist, who typified the coming of Elijah before the day of the Lord (see Mt 3:3; 11:10–14; 17:9–13; Mk 1:2–3; 9:10–13; Lk 1:17; 3:4–6; Jn 1:23). Another aspect awaits the appearance of Elijah himself before the second advent of Christ (3:2–3). The last of the Old Testament prophets anticipated the coming of the first of the New Testament prophets, John the Baptist, but there would be a four–hundred–year prophetic silence between them.

READ MALACHI 4

Prayer: *Lord, thank you that for those who fear your name, the sun of righteousness will rise with healing in its wings. Your name, O Lord, will be great among the nations.*

Meditation passage for today: verse 2

Day 208—Matthew 5

Matthew is the first of the five historical books (the Gospels and Acts) that make up 60 percent of the New Testament. These books lay the foundation upon which the epistles are built, and they show how the life of Christ and the Acts of the Apostles are embedded in a historical context. The Gospel of Matthew stresses the lordship of Christ and his perfect fulfillment of many Old Testament messianic passages. It is a portrait of Jesus that invites us to respond in humility and obedience to his loving authority.

Matthew began his account of the presentation and rejection of Israel's Messiah and King by unveiling the credentials of Jesus as the direct descendant of David, the King of the Jews sought by the Magi, the fulfillment of John the Baptist's preaching, and the sinless One who overcame the satanic temptations in the wilderness (chapters 1–4). In his matchless Sermon on the Mount (chapters 5–7), Jesus teaches that God looks at the heart and not merely our actions.

READ MATTHEW 5

Prayer: *Lord, let my light shine before others in such a way that they may see my good works and glorify my Father who is in heaven.*

Meditation passage for today: verses 3–10, 16–18

Day 209—Matthew 6

The four Gospels are not biographies but thematic portraits of Jesus Christ that are addressed to particular audiences and stress distinct aspects of the life of Christ. These unique portraits combine to create a composite picture in which the total is greater than the sum of the parts.

In Matthew 6, Jesus told his listeners that when they give, pray, and fast, they should do these things to please God rather than impress people. In his model prayer and in his teaching on anxiety, Jesus stressed the need to focus first on the Father and to look to him for every good thing.

READ MATTHEW 6

Prayer: *Lord, hallowed be your name. Your kingdom come, your will be done, on earth as it is in heaven. May I store up treasures in heaven by seeking first your kingdom and righteousness.*

Meditation passage for today: verses 9–13, 20–21, 24, 33–34

Day 210—Matthew 7

In this last portion of his Sermon on the Mount, Jesus exhorted us to examine ourselves when we are tempted to have a censorious attitude toward others. He invited us to ask, seek, and knock so that we will receive the things we need from our Father in heaven. He encapsulated the Law and the prophets in his commandment to treat people the same way we want them to treat us.

Jesus brought this sermon to a climax when he urged his listeners not merely to hear but to act upon his words. Only by entrusting ourselves to him will we be founded on the rock.

READ MATTHEW 7

Prayer: *Lord, grant me the grace to seek you, to enter through the narrow gate, and to build my house upon the rock of Christ.*

Meditation passage for today: verses 1, 7–8, 12

Day 211—Matthew 13

The Sermon on the Mount is followed by a collection of miracles that reveal Jesus' authority over nature, disease, demons, and death. Thus, his words were authenticated by his works (chapters 8–10). As the people heard Jesus' words and saw his works, the religious leaders began to oppose him. This theme of mounting rejection was developed until it culminated in the Crucifixion. In response to this opposition, Jesus began to speak in parables and spent more time with his disciples to prepare them in light of his coming death and resurrection (chapters 11–20).

In Matthew 13, Jesus used parables to conceal the truth from those who would reject it and to reveal the truth to those to whom it was granted to receive the mysteries of the kingdom of heaven.

READ MATTHEW 13

Prayer: *Lord, your Word says that your kingdom is like a treasure hidden in the field and like a pearl of great value. May I give everything I have in exchange for your kingdom and righteousness.*

Meditation passage for today: verses 11–12, 44–46

Day 212—Matthew 17

Matthew built a solid case that Jesus fulfilled the qualifications for Israel's Messiah in his lineage, his healing ministry, and his teachings. The apostle did this by using nearly 130 Old Testament quotations and allusions, more than are found in any other New Testament book.

The expression "what was spoken through the prophet was fulfilled" recurs nine times in this Gospel but does not appear in the other three Gospels. This is a book of fulfillment, in which Jesus as the Christ or Messiah uniquely fulfilled the messianic prophecies of the Hebrew Bible and offered himself to Israel as her King. This is seen in the phrase "the kingdom of heaven," which appears thirty-two times in Matthew and is found nowhere else in the New Testament. This is an important theme, because the Jewish reader would wonder why Jesus did not overthrow the Romans and establish the promised kingdom if he was indeed Israel's Messiah.

READ MATTHEW 17

Prayer: *Lord, you veiled your preincarnate glory and humbled yourself in your incarnation, your servant ministry, and your redemptive death. I rejoice that the story does not end there but continues with your glorious resurrection, your ascension, your second coming, and your eternal kingdom.*

Meditation passage for today: verses 5, 22–23

Day 213—Matthew 21

More than any of the other Gospels, Matthew emphasized the Jewish background of the life of Christ and
assumed his readers had a detailed knowledge of the Hebrew
Bible and of Jewish customs and religious traditions. Matthew
also stressed the teachings of Jesus, and 60 percent of its 1,071
verses contain his spoken words. These include two of the
three major discourses of our Lord, the Sermon on the Mount
(chapters 5–7) and the Olivet Discourse (chapters 24–25); the
third is the Upper Room Discourse in John 13–17. This Gospel
is highly structured with thematically arranged sections that
present Jesus' miracles, parables, questions, and discourses. It
converges on the central theme of mounting opposition by
the religious leaders to the Person of Jesus. Their rejection of
his offer led to the climax of the book, in his death, burial,
and resurrection.

READ MATTHEW 21

Prayer: *Lord, may the example of Jesus, who endured such hostility by
sinners against himself, teach me not to grow weary and lose heart. I give
thanks that you loved us so much that you sent your Son, and I am
grateful for his loving obedience to your will.*

Meditation passage for today: verses 5, 9, 21–22

Day 214—Matthew 24

After his triumphal entry into Jerusalem, Jesus primarily addressed those who had rejected their rightful King. He predicted the downfall of the city and the dispersion of the Jewish people among the nations as well as the events associated with his second coming as Judge and Lord (chapters 21–25). The Gospel culminates in the Crucifixion, the supreme act of rejection (chapters 26–27), and the Resurrection, God's supreme act of vindication and exaltation (chapter 28).

In this first part of the Olivet Discourse, Jesus anticipated the destruction of Jerusalem that would take place in A.D. 70, looked beyond this to speak of an unprecedented time of tribulation, and exhorted all to be ready for his second advent.

READ MATTHEW 24

Prayer: *Lord, heaven and earth will pass away, but your words will not pass away. May I heed your words and live in readiness as I anticipate your coming.*

Meditation passage for today: verses 14, 21–24, 35

Day 215—Matthew 25

The Olivet Discourse continues with two parables that illustrate the judgment of Israel and the need to be on the alert in view of the certain coming of the King. Those like the foolish virgins who only professed to be ready to meet the bridegroom will not enter the kingdom, and those like the slave who buried the talent that was given him will be excluded from the joy of their master.

When the King comes and sits upon the glorious throne of David, all the nations will be gathered before him, and he will judge the people of the earth. The sheep are those who receive the gospel and serve Jesus by serving his people, and the goats are those who reject the gospel of the kingdom.

READ MATTHEW 25

Prayer: *Lord, may I serve you by serving the people you love. By your grace, may I hear your words, "Well done, good and faithful slave. You were faithful with a few things, I will put you in charge of many things; enter into the joy of your master."*

Meditation passage for today: verses 13, 21, 31, 40

Day 216—Matthew 26

Matthew 26–27 portrays the betrayal, arrest, trial, and crucifixion of Israel's rejected King. Once again Jesus predicted his crucifixion, and the chief priests and elders plotted together to kill him. The anointing of his head by Mary of Bethany and his betrayal by Judas anticipated his impending death. It is significant that his death took place at the time of the Jewish Passover, thus linking the messianic Son of Man with the Paschal lamb. At the Lord's Supper, Jesus connected his death to the new covenant and predicted that his disciples would leave him. After the agony of Gethsemane, the Lord was betrayed by Judas, abandoned by his disciples, denied by Peter, and brought before Caiaphas and the Sanhedrin, where he was accused of blasphemy for claiming to be the Son of God.

READ MATTHEW 26

Prayer: *Lord, I am amazed at the vastness of your love, which endured rejection by your people, betrayal and abandonment by your disciples, and the agony of anticipating the awful burden of taking the cumulative sins of the world upon yourself.*

Meditation passage for today: verses 26–29

Day 217—Matthew 27

The combined Gospel accounts reveal that Jesus endured six trials. The first three were religious (before Annas, Caiaphas, and the Sanhedrin), and the last three were civil (before Pilate, Herod, and again before Pilate). When Judas realized the outcome of the deliberations, he threw the blood money into the temple, and later he hanged himself. Jesus was brought before Pilate, and after his encounter with Jesus, the governor was unsuccessful in his attempt to release him. After he was handed over, Jesus was scourged, mocked, spat upon, and beaten by the Roman soldiers, then led to the place of crucifixion outside the city walls. After the pain and humiliation of the Crucifixion, Jesus yielded up his spirit and was buried in Joseph of Arimathea's tomb.

READ MATTHEW 27

Prayer: *Lord, it is impossible for me to grasp the fullness of this mystery, that the eternal Son of God would endure such rejection, humiliation, sorrow, and agony to reconcile sinful people to you. I thank you for the new covenant with you that purchased us through your blood.*

Meditation passage for today: verses 46, 54

Day 218—Matthew 28

This glorious account of the empty tomb, the Resurrection, and the appearances of Jesus to his disciples authenticates his words and works and demonstrates that Jesus Christ is indeed the prophesied Messiah and King. The tomb had been sealed and guarded, but the angel of the Lord rolled away the stone and told the women who had come to the tomb that it was empty. They encountered the resurrected Lord on their way to tell the disciples that he had risen from the dead, and Jesus told them to have the disciples leave for Galilee, where they would see him. The guards went to the Jewish elders and were paid to say that the disciples stole the body. When the disciples later saw Jesus in Galilee, he gave them the Great Commission to make disciples of the nations.

READ MATTHEW 28

Prayer: *Lord, all authority has been given to your Son in heaven and on earth. May I be actively involved in his Great Commission to proclaim the good news to others and help others grow in his grace.*

Meditation passage for today: verses 18–20

Day 219—Mark 6

The Gospel of Mark is the most clear and concise of the four Gospels. It uses a quick-paced narrative style to tell the story of the suffering Servant, who constantly engaged in other-centered ministry through healing, teaching, and preaching. This is a book that stresses the power of servant-hood and the reality of finding our life by losing it for Christ's sake, just as he gave his life for our sake. Like the other Gospels, Mark disproportionately emphasizes the final week of the earthly life of Christ, with 40 percent of his material dedicated to the last eight days.

Chapters 1–4 emphasize the words of the Son of God, while chapters 5–7 focus more on his works. In chapter 6, Jesus taught at Nazareth, sent out the twelve, fed the multitude, walked on the water, and healed the sick wherever he encountered them.

READ MARK 6

Prayer: *Lord, you identified with us in our humanity through the humility and servanthood of the Incarnation. I give thanks for this and for the way you also demonstrated your complete authority over nature, disease, demons, and death.*

Meditation passages for today: verses 4, 31, 34, 51–52, 56

Day 220—Mark 8

Like the other Gospels, Mark is not a biography but a thematic narrative that approaches the life of Christ from a specific perspective. The theme of this Gospel is evident in Christ's clear purpose statement in 10:45: "For even the Son of Man did not come to be served, but to serve, and to give his life as a ransom for many." The eighteen miracles in Mark demonstrate not only the compassion of the Lord but also his power and authority. The miracles authenticate his teachings, which are interspersed throughout.

Jesus responded to mounting opposition by intensifying his teaching and preparation of his disciples so that they would be prepared for his departure. In the period between Mark 8:27 and Mark 10:52 (approximately six months), Jesus told his disciples of his coming death and resurrection with increasing frequency as he turned his steps toward Jerusalem.

READ MARK 8

Prayer: *Lord, may I be willing to come after Jesus by denying myself, taking up my cross, and following him. May I find life by losing it for your sake and the gospel's.*

Meditation passage for today: verses 2, 27–29, 34–38

Day 221—Luke 1

L uke is the most comprehensive of the Gospels, and it is marked by careful chronological development and accurate historical details. It combines with Acts as the first of a lengthy two-part historical narrative that begins with the foretelling of the birth of John the Baptist and ends with Paul's first Roman imprisonment.

Luke is a beautifully written Gospel that documents the perfect humanity of Jesus and presents him as the Son of Man who seeks us out and makes it possible for us to have a life-giving relationship with him. This Gospel places a strong emphasis on the ancestry, birth, and early years of the perfect man and of his forerunner John the Baptist. Their infancy stories are intertwined as Luke records their birth announcements, advents, and temple presentations.

READ LUKE 1

Prayer: *Lord, I delight in Mary's response to Gabriel's announcement, "Behold, the bondslave of the Lord; may it be done according to your word." I ask for the grace to respond to your perfect will in humility, trust, and obedience.*

Meditation passage for today: verses 17, 30–38, 42–55, 76–79

Day 222—Luke 2

Not only is Luke the longest of the four Gospels, but it is also the longest book in the New Testament. When this Gospel is combined with Acts, it constitutes 28 percent of the New Testament. Luke is also the most historically detailed of the Gospels; his refined literary Greek is rivaled only by Hebrews in the New Testament. His extensive vocabulary and wide range of expressions enhance this book. The four hymns in chapters 1 and 2 have added immensely to Christian worship (these are the *Magnificat* of Mary in 1:46–55, the *Benedictus* of Zechariah in 1:67–79, the *Gloria in Excelsis* of the heavenly host in 2:14, and the *Nunc Dimittis* of Simeon in 2:28–32).

READ LUKE 2

Prayer: *Lord, I thank you for the good news of great joy in Christ the Lord, our Savior, Redeemer, Advocate, and King.*

Meditation passage for today: verses 10–14, 29–32, 52

Day 223—Luke 4

Jesus prepared over thirty years (summarized in Luke 2:52) for a public ministry of only three years. After the infancy narratives and summary of the ministry of Jesus' forerunner, John the Baptist, the ancestry of the Son of Man is traced back to the first man, Adam. Just before Jesus launched his public ministry, he was baptized by John and led into the wilderness by the Holy Spirit, where he encountered the powerful temptations of Satan.

Like the first Adam, Christ (the last Adam) was tempted by the lust of the flesh, the lust of the eyes, and the boastful pride of life (see 1 Jn 2:16). Unlike the first Adam, our Lord resisted the devil. Early in his ministry, he was rejected by the people of his hometown, Nazareth. Beginning in Capernaum, Jesus demonstrated his authority over the realms of demons, disease, nature, and human traditions (4:31–6:49).

READ LUKE 4

Prayer: *Lord, I am grateful for Jesus' willingness to endure temptation, rejection, spiritual warfare, and physical weariness in order to accomplish his purpose of preaching the kingdom of God.*

Meditation passage for today: verses 32, 36, 41, 43

Day 224—Luke 7

As Jesus progressed in his ministry of preaching, healing, and demonic expulsion, he encountered the dual response of growing belief and growing rejection. Luke placed particular stress on the perfect humanity as well as the kindness and compassion of Jesus. His concern for all classes and conditions of people (poor and wealthy, women, Jews, Samaritans, Gentiles, tax collectors, and religious leaders) is especially evident in this book. Luke portrayed Christ's solidarity with the human condition in his identification with the sorrowful and sinful plight of people.

In Luke 9:51 Jesus commenced his last journey to Jerusalem, and in light of mounting opposition, he prepared his disciples for his departure by teaching them and building his life into them.

READ LUKE 7

Prayer: *Lord, I marvel at the compassion, gentleness, and grace of your Son, who healed the blind, the lame, the lepers, and the deaf; who raised up the dead; who preached good news to the poor; and who offered forgiveness to sinners.*

Meditation passage for today: verses 22, 47–50

Day 225—Luke 15

This remarkable chapter presents three parables that illustrate the same theme. The parables of the lost sheep, the lost coin, and the lost son were Jesus' response to the criticism of the Pharisees and the scribes that he received sinners and ate with them. In each story, something valuable was lost, an effort was made to find it, and there was rejoicing and celebration when it was restored. These stories point to the joy in heaven when one sinner repents and turns to God.

The parable of the Prodigal Son reveals an especially poignant description of God as a loving Father who waits for his wayward child to return. Seeing his son in the distance, he ran after him, embraced him, and kissed him.

READ LUKE 15

Prayer: *Lord, when I was lost and dead in my trespasses and sins, you sought me and found me. I treasure your embrace and know that I am only at home when I am with you.*

Meditation passage for today: verses 7, 10, 20, 24, 32

Day 226—Luke 16

The parable of the unrighteous steward is a surprising illustration of the fact that the children of this world are shrewder in relation to their own kind than the children of light. This story teaches us to leverage the temporal assets of time, talent, and treasure to build up people, since relationships centered on others are the currency of heaven. Jesus calls us to treat things according to their true value by pursuing the things he declares to be important. The story of the rich man and Lazarus also illustrates the need to live our lives in light of eternity instead of giving ourselves in exchange for that which is passing away.

READ LUKE 16

Prayer: *Lord, what is highly esteemed among men is often detestable in your sight. May I devote myself to you as your servant and turn away from the folly of chasing after earthly wealth.*

Meditation passage for today: verses 8–10, 13, 15, 31

Day 227—Luke 18

As he continued on his final journey to Jerusalem, Jesus instructed his disciples on a number of practical matters, including covetousness, readiness, repentance, the kingdom of God, salvation, evangelism, discipleship, forgiveness, faithfulness, humility, gratitude, the second coming, prayer, and wealth.

Jesus encouraged his disciples to be diligent and persistent in their prayers. He contrasted the futility of works based on righteousness with the need to approach God in a humble and childlike manner. And he assured his disciples that they will be disproportionately rewarded for whatever they have given up for his sake.

READ LUKE 18

Prayer: *Lord, may I never put my trust in my own efforts to attain righteousness or view other people with contempt. I ask for a spirit of humility that looks to your grace instead of my own achievements.*

Meditation passage for today: verses 1, 14, 16–17, 29–30

Day 228—Luke 19

A s the Lord entered Jericho on his way to Jerusalem, he transformed the life of a wealthy tax collector by giving Zaccheus the gift of salvation. Jesus encapsulated his ministry purpose in his declaration that "the Son of Man has come to seek and to save that which was lost."

The parable of the minas (talents) illustrates the truth that reward in the kingdom of God is not determined by what we have been given but by faithfulness in how we use what God has entrusted to us.

In his triumphal entry into Jerusalem, Jesus presented himself as Israel's promised Messiah. Seeing the city, he wept over it, knowing that it would be destroyed because of Israel's rejection of her King who had come in the name of the Lord.

READ LUKE 19

Prayer: *Lord, I desire to be faithful with all that you have given to me, knowing that I will one day give an account to you.*

Meditation passage for today: verses 10, 26, 38, 42

Day 229—Luke 20

After cleansing the temple by driving out those who were exploiting it for financial gain, the Lord encountered the opposition. It came from the chief priests, scribes, elders, and Sadducees as they sought to discredit Jesus with challenging questions. They questioned his authority, tried to snare him on the issue of paying taxes to Caesar, and attempted to defeat him with a theological dilemma concerning the resurrection. After Jesus refuted his opponents on each of these issues, he ended with a challenge of his own concerning their understanding of the Messiah that left them speechless.

READ LUKE 20

Prayer: *Father, I marvel at the poise, brilliance, courage, wisdom, and insight of the Lord Jesus. May I never be so foolish as to question his authority or intentions in my life.*

Meditation passage for today: verses 17–18, 25–26, 38

Day 230—Luke 24

As he was teaching in the temple area, Jesus told his disciples not only about the coming destruction of the temple and the city of Jerusalem but also about the signs that would precede his second advent. At the Passover meal in the Upper Room, the Lord spoke of the new covenant in his blood and once again predicted his betrayal, death, and coming kingdom. After his struggle in the Garden of Gethsemane, Jesus was betrayed, arrested, tried, and crucified.

Luke 24 concludes the narrative with the fulfillment of the glorious resurrection predicted in the Hebrew Bible and promised by Jesus. In the beautiful story of the road to Emmaus, the resurrected Jesus revealed himself to two disciples after explaining to them the messianic prophecies of Scripture.

READ LUKE 24

Prayer: *Lord, thank you for fulfilling the prophecies that the Messiah would suffer and rise again from the dead the third day, and that repentance for forgiveness of sins would be proclaimed in his name to all the nations.*

Meditation passage for today: verses 5–7, 25–27, 32, 39, 44–47

Day 231—John 1

Matthew, Mark, and Luke are known collectively as the Synoptic ("seeing together") Gospels, because they share a common viewpoint and similar material. John, on the other hand, is a supplemental Gospel, providing a wealth of stories and teachings of Jesus that are not found in the synoptics. The Synoptic Gospels, for example, focus on Christ's Galilean ministry, while John develops his Judean ministry.

The prologue (1:1–18) is one of the richest theological texts in Scripture. It reveals the eternality and divinity of the Word as well as the incarnation of the Word. This prologue is followed by an account of the witness of John the Baptist concerning Jesus and the story of Jesus' first disciples (1:19–51).

READ JOHN 1

Prayer: *Lord, thank you for the mystery of the Word who became flesh and dwelt among us. I am grateful that while the Law was given through Moses, grace and truth were realized through Jesus Christ.*

Meditation passage for today: verses 1–5, 10–18, 51

Day 232—John 3

Chapters 2–12 present seven attesting signs that point to the Person and life-giving power of Jesus:

(1) turning the water into wine (2:1–11);

(2) healing the royal official's son (4:46–54);

(3) healing the invalid (5:1–15);

(4) feeding the multitude (6:1–14);

(5) walking on water (6:16–21);

(6) giving sight to the man born blind (9:1–41); and

(7) the raising of Lazarus (11:1–45).

In most cases, John follows these signs with a presentation of the reactions of belief and disbelief.

The story of Jesus' interview with Nicodemus points to the human need to be born of the Spirit in order to enjoy life with God. In John's testimony to Jesus, he saw himself as the friend of the bridegroom and affirmed that "he must increase, but I must decrease." This is the essence of the spiritual life.

READ JOHN 3

Prayer: Lord, your gift of eternal life to all who believe in your Son is the highest expression of your unbounded love for us. I ask that in my life, Jesus would increase and I would decrease.

Meditation passage for today: verses 3, 5–8, 14–21, 30, 35–36

Day 233—John 4

O ur Lord always adapted himself perfectly and graciously to the people he encountered. In John 3 he challenged Nicodemus to revisit the knowledge he should have had as a "teacher of Israel." But in John 4 he gradually revealed his true nature to an obscure woman at a well in Samaria. Even in speaking to her, Jesus overcame three barriers: first, the racial barrier (Jews had no dealings with Samaritans), second, the gender barrier (Jewish rabbis would not address women as Jesus did), and third, the social barrier (this woman had a poor reputation among her own people). Jesus knew everything she had done, and yet he gently and lovingly offered her the living water of eternal life.

READ JOHN 4

Prayer: *Lord, I give thanks that you know me through and through, and still you love me and desire intimacy with me. Give me the grace of holy desire so that I will respond eagerly to your gracious and loving initiatives.*

Meditation passage for today: verses 10, 13–14, 23–24

Day 234—John 6

The seven "I am" statements in John's Gospel combine to provide a profound portrait of the Lord Jesus:

- "I am the bread of life" (6:35);
- "I am the light of the world" (8:12; 9:5);
- "I am the door of the sheep" (10:7, 9);
- "I am the good shepherd" (10:11, 14);
- "I am the resurrection and the life" (11:25);
- "I am the way, the truth, and the life" (14:6); and
- "I am the true vine" (15:1–5).

Jesus listed five witnesses in 5:30–40 that bear witness to his authority and deity, and one of these witnesses is "the works which the Father has given me to accomplish." The feeding of the multitude, recorded in all four Gospels, is a clear witness to the Person and power of Jesus, but his discourse on the Bread of Life caused many to leave him when he related this bread to his flesh.

READ JOHN 6

Prayer: *Lord, I anchor my hope in your promise that those who come to you will not hunger, and those who believe in you will never thirst. Everyone who beholds your Son and believes in him will have eternal life, and he will raise them up on the last day.*

Meditation passage for today: verses 27–29, 35–40, 51, 68–69

Day 235–John 8

While all of the Gospels are thematic portraits, John is by far the most theological and selective. It also has the most unique material: 42 percent of Matthew, 7 percent of Mark, and 59 percent of Luke is unique to these Gospels, but 92 percent of John is unique to John.

In his narratives, John symbolically developed the theme of how those who were exposed to Jesus' words and works responded by either accepting or rejecting him. Those who receive him have eternal life (1:12; 3:16; 5:24; 10:27–29), while those who reject his offer remain under the condemnation of God (3:36; 5:25–29; 8:24). Jesus' controversy with his opponents in John 8 illustrates this rejection and ends with their attempt to stone him when he associated himself with the divine I AM of the Old Testament (8:58; cf. 4:25–26; 8:24, 28; 13:19; 18:5–6, 8).

READ JOHN 8

Prayer: *Lord, when I entrust myself to you, you set me free from my slavery to sin and make me your child forever. Thank you.*

Meditation passage for today: verses 12, 24, 28, 34–36, 58

Day 236—John 10

The vocabulary and grammatical structure of the Gospel of John is simpler than the other Gospels, but this Gospel is more subtle and layered, and it is full of nuances and parallelism. While the synoptics all contain Jesus' parables, John uses allegories instead (for example, the Good Shepherd in John 10 and the True Vine in John 15).

In his allegory of the Good Shepherd, Jesus presented himself as the gate by which the sheep may enter, the shepherd who is concerned for his flock and protects them, the one who knows his sheep and whose sheep know him, and the lover of the flock who lays down his life for them. The Father is in him, and he is in the Father. The Father sent him into the world to purchase eternal life for the sheep his Father had given to him.

READ JOHN 10

Prayer: *Lord, you are my shepherd, and I belong to your flock. Help me to look to you for all my needs, knowing that it is you who guide me, feed me, protect me, and give me the gift of eternal and abundant life.*

Meditation passage for today: verses 7–11, 14–15, 18, 27–30

Day 237—John 13

In view of increasing hostility to his words and works, Jesus saw that his hour had finally come. At his last supper with the disciples, he prepared them for his imminent departure (chapters 13–16) and interceded for them (chapter 17). The Upper Room Discourse, recorded only in John, is the most complete of Jesus' messages, and it contains the seed themes concerning the spiritual life that are later developed in the epistles.

Jesus, who loved and served his own until the end, gave his disciples a new commandment to love one another, even as he loved them. Having washed the feet of his disciples (including Judas), Jesus predicted his betrayal. After Judas went out into the night, the Lord told his disciples of his imminent departure from this world.

READ JOHN 13

Prayer: *Lord, grant me your power to love others even as you have loved me. May the love of the believers in my community be a demonstration that we are your disciples.*

Meditation passage for today: verses 1, 3, 13–15, 34–35

Day 238—John 14

In this portion of his Upper Room Discourse, Jesus prepared his disciples for his departure to the Father. He assured them of his continuing presence in their lives through the ongoing ministry of the Spirit of truth. He told his own that he would prepare a place for them and then come again to receive them to himself. Jesus exhorted them to love him and keep his words so that he and the Father would love them and make their abode with them. The deep mystery contained in the seven words "You in me, and I in you" speaks of the mutual indwelling that is the central truth and dynamic of the spiritual life. Jesus promised them a transcendent source of peace that could overcome their anxieties.

READ JOHN 14

Prayer: *Lord, thank you for your gift of the abiding Holy Spirit, for your comforting words in a world of anxiety, for your glorious promises, and for loving your own and disclosing yourself to us.*

Meditation passage for today: verses 1–6, 11–15, 20–21, 23, 27

Day 239—John 15

As Jesus led his disciples to the Garden of Gethsemane, he related the allegory of the vine and the branches to teach them about their need to abide in him for their spiritual sustenance. It was only as they abided in him that they would be empowered to bear fruit. It is this fruit that would demonstrate their discipleship. Once again, Jesus commanded them to love one another just as he loved them, and he emphasized that it was not they who chose him, but he who chose them. Due to their identification with him, Jesus warned his disciples that the world would persecute them as it persecuted him.

READ JOHN 15

Prayer: *Father, you are the vinedresser, Jesus is the True Vine, and I am a branch that desires to receive Christ's life by abiding in him. May I abide in your love, keep your commandments, and love others as you have loved me.*

Meditation passage for today: verses 1–17

Day 240—John 16

Knowing that the time of his suffering and death was at hand, Jesus told his disciples of the Holy Spirit, who would equip them with perspective and power in their ministries after Jesus returned to the Father. The Holy Spirit would come to them, guide them into all the truth, and convict the world concerning sin, righteousness, and judgment.

The Lord also prepared the disciples for the suffering they would experience because of their testimony about him. Though they would experience grief after his departure, he assured them that their grief would turn into joy when they saw him again. In response, the disciples declared their faith in Jesus, professing their belief that he had come from God.

READ JOHN 16

Prayer: *Lord, it is in you that I find true joy and peace. During my times of tribulation in this world teach me to take courage, because Jesus has overcome the world.*

Meditation passage for today: verses 7–14, 23–24, 28, 33

Day 241—John 17

In this chapter, we are privileged to enter the most holy place of loving communion between the Father and the Son. In this high priestly prayer, offered just prior to the anguish of the Garden and the events that followed, Jesus interceded on behalf of his disciples as well as those who believe in him.

As he was about to leave the world, Jesus lifted up those who had been given to him, asking his Father to "keep them in your name, the name which you have given me, that they may be one even as we are." Just as he was in the Father and the Father was in him, so the Lord prayed that those who believed in him would be perfected in unity and experience the mystery of "I in them, and you in me."

READ JOHN 17

Prayer: *Lord, thank you that you prayed for us to be unified. Thank you that this unity is possible by your dwelling in us.*

Meditation passage for today: verses 3–4, 11, 16–18, 21–26

Day 242—John 20

A fter a gripping account of Jesus' arrest, trials, and cruci-fixion (chapters 18–19), John provides a vivid narrative of several post–Resurrection encounters between the Lord and his disciples (chapters 20–21). John's purpose statement is the clearest in Scripture: "But these have been written so that you may believe that Jesus is the Christ, the Son of God; and that believing you may have life in his name" (20:31). The beloved disciple selected the seven miraculous signs in chapters 1–12 and the Resurrection in chapters 20–21 to bring the reader into an understanding of who Jesus is and to elicit a response of personal trust in him.

Jesus' post–Resurrection appearances to Mary Magdalene, the disciples without Thomas, and the disciples with Thomas were a source of unspeakable joy.

READ JOHN 20

Prayer: *Lord, I have believed that Jesus is the Christ, the Son of God, and I have found life in his name. As you have sent him, so he also sends me.*

Meditation passage for today: verses 17, 19–21, 26–31

Day 243—John 21

At his meeting with the disciples at the Sea of Galilee, Jesus restored Peter and commissioned him to shepherd his sheep. John's Gospel concludes by alluding to the abundance of things Jesus did that were never recorded.

As topical narratives, each of the four Gospels approaches the life of Christ from a different angle. Matthew presents him to a Jewish readership as Israel's Messiah-King, Mark presents him to a Roman readership as the Servant-Redeemer, and Luke presents him to a Greek readership as the Perfect Man.

John, evidently written after the three Synoptic Gospels, presents Christ to a universal readership as the Son of God. The traditional picture of Christ in the four Gospels relates to the imagery in Ezekiel 1:10 and Revelation 4:6-8 and is as follows: Matthew, a lion (strength, authority); Mark, an ox (service, power); Luke, a man (wisdom, character); John, an eagle (divinity).

READ JOHN 21

Prayer: *Lord, thank you for this marvelous account of Jesus' encounter with his disciples at the Sea of Galilee. I ask for the grace to follow Jesus wherever he leads me.*

Meditation passage for today: verses 15–17, 25

Day 244—Acts 1

In the Great Commission (see Mt 28:19–20), Jesus' followers were instructed to go and make disciples of all nations. This commission was supplemented by Christ's last words to his disciples before his ascension into heaven: "But you will receive power when the Holy Spirit has come upon you; and you shall be my witnesses in Jerusalem, and in all Judea and Samaria, and even to the remotest part of the earth" (1:8).

Luke wrote Acts to provide a historical link between the Gospels and the epistles and to chronicle the key events that brought about the birth and rapid spread of the church, beginning in Jerusalem and moving beyond the borders of Israel to the other provinces of the Roman Empire.

The resurrected Lord instructed his disciples to wait in Jerusalem for the Holy Spirit to come and empower them to be his witnesses. After Jesus ascended into heaven, the disciples chose Matthias to replace Judas as an apostle.

READ ACTS 1

Prayer: *Lord, it is your Holy Spirit who empowers me to be your witness to the people in my sphere of influence. May I live in such a way that they will be attracted to Jesus.*

Meditation passage for today: verses 3–8

Day 245—Acts 2

A cts continues the story of the birth of Christianity from the ascension of Christ to the time of Paul's first imprisonment in Rome. It serves as a crucial historical narrative that provides the backdrop to most of the epistles as it develops the exciting story of the birth and expansion of the early church.

When the Holy Spirit came on the Day of Pentecost, Peter was empowered to deliver a sermon about the resurrected Christ that led to the conversion of three thousand listeners. All the sermons and defenses in Acts point to Jesus Christ as the resurrected Savior of the world. In his sermon in Acts 2, Peter built upon Jesus' fulfillment of several Old Testament passages and pointed his listeners to the fact of the empty tomb to convict them that Jesus is both Lord and Christ (2:36).

READ ACTS 2

Prayer: *Lord, only the resurrection of Jesus and the indwelling power of the Holy Spirit can account for this radical transformation in the life of Peter. May I abide in the same hope and power.*

Meditation passage for today: verses 22–24, 36–38, 42

Day 246—Acts 7

After healing a man who was lame from birth, Peter delivered a convicting message to the people and another to the Sanhedrin (chapters 3–4). The church continued to grow, but the apostles were persecuted because of their message (chapter 5). Deacons were appointed to assist the apostles (chapter 6), and one of them, Stephen, spoke with such wisdom and authority that he was dragged before the Sanhedrin to be condemned.

In his defense before the Jewish rulers, Stephen reviewed the biblical narrative from the call of Abraham to the time of David and Solomon. Both Joseph and Moses were initially rejected by their people and later vindicated as God's deliverers. Stephen charged that in the same way, the people had resisted the Holy Spirit by rejecting Jesus as their Messiah.

READ ACTS 7

Prayer: *Lord, by your grace, may I not resist the work of the Holy Spirit in my life. I want to embrace your good purposes for me and submit to your loving authority.*

Meditation passage for today: verses 55–56, 59–60

Day 247—Acts 8

Philip, another of the deacons selected in Acts 6, was led to proclaim Christ to the Samaritans, who were viewed with disdain by the Jews. Philip's message was accompanied by attesting signs, and Simon the magician was attracted by these works of power. The apostles in Jerusalem sent Peter and John to Samaria to confer the gift of the Holy Spirit upon these new believers, but when Simon sought to buy the authority to impart this gift, Peter rebuked him for his wicked intentions.

Philip was directed by an angel to go to a desert road where he encountered an Ethiopian court official who was reading the messianic prophecy in Isaiah 53. When Philip preached Jesus to him, he believed and was baptized.

READ ACTS 8

Prayer: *Lord, your goodness and salvation extend to all who call upon your name. May I be ready and faithful to share the good news about your Son as your Spirit gives me opportunity.*

Meditation passage for today: verses 34–37

Day 248—Acts 9

S aul, an approving witness of the martyrdom of Stephen (7:58; 8:1–3), was a young Pharisee who zealously ravaged the church in his opposition to followers of the Way. Not content with persecuting those who believed in Jesus in Judea, Saul obtained authority to go to Damascus to bring these followers of Jesus to trial in Jerusalem. Saul's life was radically and permanently changed after his encounter with the resurrected Jesus on the road to Damascus, and he soon began to proclaim Jesus in the synagogues as the Son of God. Saul ministered for a time in Jerusalem, until he was endangered and sent away to Tarsus.

The narrative switches back to Peter and relates the story of his healing of Aeneas in Lydda and his raising of Tabitha from the dead in Joppa.

READ ACTS 9

Prayer: *Lord, I thank you for the way you miraculously converted Saul. I thank you that you made your salvation available to all.*

Meditation passage for today: verses 15–16, 31

Day 249—Acts 10

The gospel of the resurrected Christ was first proclaimed to the Jews in Jerusalem and Judea, and then reached the Samaritan people. This crucial chapter records the first reception of the gospel among the Gentiles and marks the decisive point where Jews and Gentiles both become members of one body in Christ.

The Roman centurion Cornelius was a God-fearing man whose prayers and alms led to an angelic visitation in which he was instructed to dispatch men to Joppa to send for Peter. Meanwhile, Peter received three visions that prepared him to go willingly with the messengers to the house of Cornelius, where he proclaimed that everyone who believes in Jesus receives forgiveness of sins. The Spirit of God came upon these Gentiles, and they were baptized in the name of Jesus Christ.

READ ACTS 10

Prayer: *Lord, the abundance of your mercy and grace is available to everyone who seeks you. I acknowledge that Jesus is the Judge of the living and the dead, and that through his name everyone who believes in him receives forgiveness of sins.*

Meditation passage for today: verses 15, 34–35, 42–43

Day 250—Acts 13

A cts is a highly selective historical account, and though it is sometimes called "The Acts of the Apostles," it is pre–dominantly a series of important acts of Peter (chapters 1–12) and of Paul (chapters 13–28). This is a transitional book that explains how the composition of the church changed from being entirely Jewish (chapters 1–7) to a body that included Samaritans and Gentiles (chapters 8–12). By the end of the twenty–nine years covered in this book, the majority of believers in Christ were Gentiles.

In chapters 13–28, Luke shifts his attention from Peter to Paul and gives an account of Paul's three missionary journeys and his trials and expedition to Rome. In the first missionary journey in A.D. 48–49 (13:1–14:28), Paul ministered in the province of Galatia.

READ ACTS 13

Prayer: *Lord, I thank you for your glorious provision of forgiveness of sins and newness of life to all who transfer their trust from their own efforts to the perfect Person and work of the Lord Jesus.*

Meditation passage for today: verses 38–39, 48, 52

Day 251—Acts 15

After his first missionary journey, Paul and his co-laborer Barnabas returned to Syrian Antioch and reported to the church what God had done among the Gentiles. When some men from Judea argued that the Gentiles could not be saved unless they became proselytes to Judaism, Paul and Barnabas were sent to the apostles and elders in Jerusalem to resolve this crucial issue. Peter argued from his own experience that salvation is a gift of God for both Jews and Gentiles through the grace of the Lord Jesus and not through keeping the Law of Moses. James concurred, and the apostles and elders sent Paul and Barnabas, along with Judas and Silas, to Antioch with a letter to confirm the council's conclusion.

READ ACTS 15

Prayer: *Lord, I give thanks that you make no distinction between people but make the same good news of forgiveness, cleansing, and grace available to all who turn to Jesus by faith.*

Meditation passage for today: verses 7–11

Day 252—Acts 16

A cts 15:36–18:22 records Paul's second missionary journey, which took place in A.D. 50–52. Paul, accompanied this time by Silas, returned to Galatia and then proceeded beyond to Macedonia and Greece. Timothy soon joined them, and they strengthened the churches that had been established earlier.

Heading north and then west, they reached Troas, where Paul had a vision of a man of Macedonia who was calling for help. Responding to this call, they headed to Macedonia and made their way to Philippi. When Paul and Silas were beaten and thrown into an inner prison, their hymns of praise to God so affected the prisoners that none escaped when given an opportunity. This remarkable event led to the conversion of the Philippian jailer and his household.

READ ACTS 16

Prayer: *Lord, thank you for the simplicity and profundity of the good news that is encapsulated in the statement, "Believe in the Lord Jesus, and you will be saved." I entrust myself to him and thank you for the gift of new life that he purchased for all who call upon your name.*

Meditation passage for today: verses 30–31

Day 253—Acts 17

After leaving Philippi, Paul, Silas, and Timothy made their way to Thessalonica; there a number of Jews and God-fearing Greeks came to faith in Jesus. The Jewish leaders stirred up the people against them, and Paul and his companions went on to Berea, where the people "received the word with great eagerness" until agitators from Thessalonica turned the crowds against Paul.

Silas and Timothy remained for a time in Berea, while Paul journeyed to Athens, where he reasoned in the synagogue and in the marketplace. When he was given an opportunity to address the Athenians on the Areopagus (Mars Hill), Paul told them about the one true God who "will judge the world in righteousness through a Man whom he has appointed, having furnished proof to all men by raising him from the dead."

READ ACTS 17

Prayer: *Lord, you give to all people life, breath, and all things; in you we live and move and exist. I give thanks that you have made it possible to know you through a relationship with your Son Christ Jesus.*

Meditation passage for today: verses 11, 24–31

Day 254—Acts 18

Paul went on from Athens to Corinth, where he continued his custom of bringing the gospel to the Jews first and then to the Gentiles. He allied himself with Aquila and his wife Priscilla, and when Silas and Timothy joined him, he devoted himself to proclaiming and teaching about Jesus the Messiah. Many of the Corinthians came to faith in Christ, and Paul spent eighteen months teaching the Word of God among them. Paul and his companions then sailed to Ephesus, where he reasoned with the Jews in the synagogue. From there he sailed to Caesarea, went up to greet the church in Jerusalem, and returned to Antioch. After a time, Paul commenced his third missionary journey (A.D. 53–57; Acts 18:23–21:16), returning first to the region of Galatia and Phrygia to strengthen the disciples.

READ ACTS 18

Prayer: *Lord, I thank you for the messianic prophecies in the Hebrew Bible that point to Jesus. May I come to know him better by abiding in him, entrusting myself to him, and affirming his lordship over every component of my life.*

Meditation passage for today: verses 5, 28

Day 255—Acts 21

Paul continued west to Ephesus, the capital city of the Roman province of Asia, where he spent over two years teaching and reasoning daily and performing miracles of healing. As the word of the Lord spread throughout Asia, Paul's opponents in Ephesus caused an uproar, and Paul decided to leave Ephesus to visit and exhort the churches in Macedonia and Greece.

After a few months, Paul and his companions made their way back to Troas, from which they sailed to Miletus, where they met with the elders of the Ephesian church. Paul solemnly exhorted them and then set sail with his friends and journeyed on to Jerusalem. When some of Paul's Jewish opponents from Asia saw him in the temple, they stirred up the crowd against him. The mob dragged him out of the temple and began beating him, until he was rescued by the soldiers under the Roman commander.

READ ACTS 21

Prayer: *Lord, Paul's passion for the gospel and his willingness to suffer deprivation, persecution, and death for the name of the Lord Jesus is both inspiring and challenging. May I be willing to endure hardship for the sake of his name.*

Meditation passage for today: verses 13–14

Day 256—Acts 22

When Paul was brought into the Roman barracks, he obtained permission from the commander to make his defense before the crowd. Addressing the people in Jewish Aramaic, Paul related how he had persecuted the followers of the Way as a zealous Pharisee until his encounter with the resurrected Jesus on the road to Damascus.

Ananias had healed Paul's blindness and told him that he would be a witness to all of what he had seen and heard. But when Paul told the crowd about his divine commission to preach to the Gentiles, the people became furious and began shouting at him. The commander ordered that Paul be returned to the barracks and examined by scourging, but he changed his mind when Paul informed him of his Roman citizenship.

READ ACTS 22

Prayer: *Lord, I am reminded that the gospel of the Lord Jesus has never been neutral, but cuts between those who seek you and those who turn away from you. May I be faithful to live for Jesus and to speak well of him regardless of how people respond.*

Meditation passage for today: verses 14–16

Day 257—Acts 23

The Roman commander ordered the Sanhedrin to convene and set Paul before them to discover why he had been accused by the Jews. As a Pharisee, Paul quickly took advantage of the division between the Sadducees and the Pharisees over the issue of the resurrection from the dead, and this immediately caused a dissension between the two parties.

Once again, the commander had to remove Paul to the safety of the Roman barracks. When Paul's nephew informed the commander of a conspiracy to kill Paul, he arranged to have Paul removed to Caesarea, where his accusers could bring charges against him before Felix, the governor. Felix read the commander's letter and arranged to give Paul a hearing after the arrival of his accusers.

READ ACTS 23

Prayer: *Lord, I take courage in the truth that no human opposition can defeat your good purposes. May I trust you in difficult times, knowing that you always have my ultimate good at heart.*

Meditation passage for today: verses 6, 11

Day 258—Acts 24

Paul's accusers arrived in Caesarea and appeared before Felix, charging that Paul was a ringleader of a sect and was stirring up dissension among the Jews.

When the governor gave Paul an opportunity to make his defense, the apostle argued that his opponents could give no proof of the charges they were making. He focused on the hope of the resurrection of the dead, a belief that is compatible with the Hebrew Scriptures.

Felix decided to wait until Lysias the commander came down to Caesarea to decide Paul's case. For the next two years, however, Felix kept Paul in custody, allowing his friends to visit him, and often sent for him to converse with him. When Paul told the governor about faith in Christ Jesus, he came under conviction, but not to the point of repentance and faith.

READ ACTS 24

Prayer: *Lord, the biblical truths about righteousness, self-control, and the judgment to come can frighten hardened and powerful people, but only your Holy Spirit can bring a person to the point of regeneration. May I rely on the power of your Spirit in my walk and witness.*

Meditation passage for today: verses 14–16, 25

Day 259—Acts 25

After two years of imprisonment in Caesarea, Paul heard that the governor, Felix, was being succeeded by Festus. When the new governor went up to Jerusalem, Paul's opponents saw this as an opportunity to bring charges against him, hoping that he would be brought to Jerusalem so they could have him killed on the way.

Festus invited them to come to Caesarea to prosecute Paul. When Paul was brought out before them, the new governor asked Paul if he was willing to stand trial in Jerusalem. Knowing what this would mean, Paul exercised his right as a Roman citizen to appeal to Caesar. When King Agrippa and Bernice arrived at Caesarea to visit Festus, the governor arranged for them to hear Paul, hoping to clarify the charges before sending the prisoner to the Emperor.

READ ACTS 25

Prayer: *Lord, the plots and devices of men will never prevail against your purposes and promises. May I imitate Paul's faith by taking the long-term perspective, and thus live by faith and hope.*

Meditation passage for today: verses 8, 11

Day 260—Acts 26

The apostle took full advantage of his opportunity to present his defense before King Agrippa and argued that the hope of the resurrection from the dead is fully in accord with the prophetic writings revered by the Jews. Paul recounted his efforts as a Pharisee to persecute the followers of Jesus of Nazareth and his encounter with Jesus himself on the way to Damascus. He then related his commission to proclaim to both Jews and Gentiles the message of forgiveness of sins through faith in Jesus. When Paul argued that Moses and the prophets predicted these things about the Messiah, Festus accused Paul of madness. The apostle appealed to Agrippa's knowledge of the Jewish prophets, but the king shrugged it off. He told Festus afterward that Paul could have been released, had he not appealed to Caesar.

READ ACTS 26

Prayer: *Lord, I give thanks for the life-giving message that turns people from darkness to light and from the dominion of Satan to God, that they may receive forgiveness of sins and an inheritance among those who have been sanctified by faith in Jesus.*

Meditation passage for today: verses 18–20, 22–23

Day 261—Acts 27

Paul and other prisoners were delivered to a Roman centurion named Julius, who made arrangements to bring them by ship to Rome. After they sailed to Lycia, Julius put his soldiers and prisoners on a ship that was bound for Italy. The trip became increasingly treacherous, and when they arrived at Crete, Paul warned them not to continue on. Hoping to make it to a suitable harbor for wintering, however, Julius decided with the majority to continue on.

Their ship was soon caught in a violent storm, and when all hope of being saved was lost, Paul related an angelic message he had received that he would stand before Caesar and that none of them would perish in the sea. Paul predicted that they would run aground on an island, and when this occurred, all of them were brought safely to land.

READ ACTS 27

Prayer: *Lord, your word never fails, and you accomplish all the things you promise to your saints. May I cling to you during the storms of life and hope in your life-giving promises.*

Meditation passage for today: verses 24–25

Day 262—Acts 28

The 276 people from the shipwreck found themselves on the island of Malta, and the natives kindled a fire to warm them against the cold and the rain. A viper bit Paul on the hand, and when they observed that he suffered no harm, the natives began to say that he was a god.

Publius generously entertained his new guests, and after Paul healed the father of Publius, the rest of the people on the island came to Paul for healing. After three months, Paul and the others embarked on a ship that had wintered at the island, and they finally arrived at the port of Puteoli in Italy, south of Rome. Paul was brought to Rome where he was placed under house arrest to await his trial before Caesar. He gathered the leading members of the Jewish community to explain his circumstances and to explain from the Scriptures that Jesus is the promised Messiah.

READ ACTS 28

Prayer: *Lord, I ask for the wisdom, the boldness, and the opportunity to testify about the kingdom of God and the Lord Jesus Christ with sensitivity and clarity.*

Meditation passage for today: verses 23, 31

Day 263—Romans 1

While the Gospels portray the words and works of Jesus Christ, Romans develops the profound implications of his life, death, and resurrection for those who trust in him. Romans is the most systematic and comprehensive theological treatise in the Bible, and it presents the powerful themes of salvation, righteousness, faith, justification, redemption, atonement, reconciliation, and imputation with greater clarity than anywhere else in Scripture. Romans 6–8 is the supreme passage for the meaning of the spiritual life, and Romans 12–14 is crucial to our understanding of the outworking of the spiritual life.

The theme of Romans, spelled out in 1:16–17, is that the gospel is the power of God for salvation and righteousness for those whose faith is in Jesus Christ.

READ ROMANS 1

Prayer: *Lord, you have revealed yourself to all people through your vast and marvelous created order. Yet so many people have turned away from the glory of the incorruptible God to worship and serve the creature. May I always honor you as God and give thanks.*

Meditation passage for today: verses 3–4, 16–20

Day 264—Romans 2

During his stay in Corinth near the end of his third missionary journey in A.D. 57, Paul wrote this magnificent epistle to the well-known and influential church in Rome, which he had not yet visited. Paul launched his epistle with a prologue that states his intention of coming to Rome as well as his theme of righteousness (conformity to God's character) before God through faith in Christ (1:1-17). He then developed an unanswerable case for the universal condemnation of both Gentiles and Jews in view of their sinful condition of falling short of the righteousness of God (1:18-3:20).

Having demonstrated the condemnation of the Gentiles in chapter 1, Paul did the same regarding both the moral Jew and the religious Jew in chapter 2. The human conscience reveals that people cannot even live up to their own moral standards.

READ ROMANS 2

Prayer: *Lord, I know that whenever I judge another, I condemn myself, since I cannot even keep my own moral standards, let alone those revealed in your Word. May I keep my eyes on your Son rather than the shortcomings of others.*

Meditation passage for today: verses 1, 14-16

Day 265—Romans 3

Having indicted both the Gentiles and the Jews, the apostle completed his portrait of universal condemnation before a holy God with a series of quotations from the Psalms. The Law demonstrates the knowledge of sin, but it does not provide a solution.

God's solution to this universal human dilemma is found in the redemption and atoning work of Jesus Christ. Faith in him rather than works is the key to appropriating his offer of grace by which we are justified (declared righteous) by God himself (3:21-31). While "all have sinned and fall short of the glory of God," we are "justified as a gift by his grace through the redemption which is in Christ Jesus."

READ ROMANS 3

Prayer: *Lord, you have paid the price of redemption through the blood of your Son. It is through faith in him that I have received the grace of being justified in your sight.*

Meditation passage for today: verses 20, 23-28

Day 266—Romans 4

Paul used the experience of David and the life of Abraham to illustrate the principle of justification by faith apart from works. It was through the righteousness of faith that Abraham was justified, and this took place prior to his circumcision. It was his faith that made him the father of all who believe, whether they are Jews or Gentiles. Abraham believed God's promise concerning his descendants ("Then he believed in the Lord; and he reckoned it to him as righteousness"; Gn 15:6), though this faith in the promise of God was contrary to human appearances. Thus, Abraham became the exemplar for all "who believe in him who raised Jesus our Lord from the dead."

READ ROMANS 4

Prayer: *Lord, I thank you for Abraham's faith in you and in your promise to him, even though it appeared impossible to fulfill. I am grateful that when I put my trust in Jesus, this faith was credited to me as righteousness.*

Meditation passage for today: verses 3–5, 17, 24–25

Day 267—Romans 5

Justification by faith leads to peace and reconciliation with God (5:1–11). Reconciliation speaks of the change in our state of alienation from God because of the redemptive work of his Son on our behalf. It is made possible through God's love, which is causeless (5:6), measureless (5:7–8), and ceaseless (5:9–11). In 5:12–21, Paul contrasts the two Adams and the opposite results of their two acts. The disobedience of the first Adam made him the head of all who are under sin, but the obedience of the Second Adam made him the head of the race of redeemed humanity. The sin of the first Adam was imputed to us (placed on our account), leading to alienation. However, the righteousness of Christ is imputed to all who trust in him, leading to reconciliation.

READ ROMANS 5

Prayer: *Lord, your love has been poured out within our hearts through the Holy Spirit who was given to us. You demonstrated your own love toward us, in that while we were yet sinners, Christ died for us.*

Meditation passage for today: verses 1–8, 20–21

Day 268—Romans 6

Romans presents Christ as the Savior and Redeemer whose atoning work on the cross has made it possible for God to "be just and the justifier of the one who has faith in Jesus" (3:26). He is the Second Adam, whose obedience has overcome the sin and separation caused by the first Adam's disobedience (5:12–21). It is through our identification with him in his death, burial, and resurrection that we enjoy freedom from the dominion of sin and newness of life (6:1–23). The reality of union with Christ is the basis for the spiritual walk. Believers must know their position in Christ, regard it as true, and present themselves to God as dead to sin but alive to God in Christ Jesus. Paul views devotion as a response to spiritual truth, not as a condition of it.

READ ROMANS 6

Prayer: *Lord, I acknowledge by faith that I have been united with your Son in his death, burial, and resurrection. I acknowledge that in Christ I am no longer a slave to sin. I present myself to you as one alive from the dead, and my members as instruments of righteousness to you.*

Meditation passage for today: verses 3–14, 23

Day 269—Romans 7

The apostle argues that the only way we can be released from the jurisdiction of the Law is to die. Our death in Christ to that by which we were bound enables us to "serve in newness of the Spirit and not in oldness of the letter." Paul states that the Mosaic Law was given in order to reveal the problem of indwelling sin and our condition of separation from the holiness of God.

In 7:14–25 Paul speaks of the conflict that believers in Christ experience between the "inner man" (the new nature we have received in Christ) and the "flesh" or "the law of sin which is in my members." This inward–outward conflict between the new and the old dispositions will not be eliminated until we are in our resurrected bodies.

READ ROMANS 7

Prayer: *Lord, I joyfully concur with the law of God in my inner being in Christ, but I see a different law in the members of my body. May I walk in union with Christ and in the power of your Spirit.*

Meditation passage for today: verses 4, 6, 22–25

Day 270—Romans 8

Followers of Christ have two present resources to give them victory in the painful inward–outward conflict described in 7:14–25. The first is our identification with Christ in his death, burial, and resurrection life (Romans 6), and the second is the indwelling presence of the Holy Spirit (Romans 8). People who have turned from their sins (repentance) and trusted in Christ (faith) are indwelled by the Spirit of him who raised Christ Jesus from the dead. When we set our minds on the Spirit, we walk in his life and peace.

Having dealt with the issues of our condemnation (1:18–3:20), our justification (3:21–5:21), and our sanctification (6:1–8:17), Paul looks ahead to our glorification (8:18–39). All believers can anticipate a time when they will be perfectly conformed to Jesus Christ not only in their position (present) but also in their practice (the future resurrection).

READ ROMANS 8

Prayer: *Lord, I praise you that neither death, nor life, nor angels, nor principalities, nor things present, nor things to come, nor powers, nor height, nor depth, nor any other created thing will be able to separate me from your love in Christ Jesus my Lord.*

Meditation passage for today: verses 1–6, 9–18, 26–30, 38–39

Day 271—Romans 12

In chapters 1-8, Paul unfolds God's sovereign plan of salvation, and in chapters 9-11, he deals with the question of God's relationship to Israel now that the Gentiles have the same access as the Jews to Israel's Messiah. The third section, chapters 12-16, focuses on the application of life in Christ to various practical aspects of daily experience.

The apostle recognized that behavior must be built upon belief, and this is why the practical exhortations of this epistle appear after his teaching on the believer's position in Christ. Personal consecration (12:1-2) should lead to corporate transformation (12:3-21); the dynamic of our faith in Christ must be expressed in other-centered relationships in the body of Christ.

READ ROMANS 12

Prayer: *Lord, because of all you have done for me, I present my body to you as a living sacrifice. I want to be transformed by the renewing of my mind, affirming that your will for me is good, acceptable, and perfect.*

Meditation passage for today: verses 1-5, 9-18

Day 272—Romans 13

The salvation described in the first eleven chapters should transform a believer's life in relation to God (12:1-2), ministry to the body of Christ (12:3-8), social relationships (12:9-21), submission to governing authorities (13:1-7), and the needs of others (13:8-15:13).

Paul argues that in spite of their flaws, governing authorities are established by God; it is he who raises them up and deposes them. Only when a government overreaches its divinely given sphere of authority can followers of Jesus stand in opposition. Romans 13 concludes with an affirmation that love is the fulfillment of the law, and with an exhortation to live in view of the future by putting on the armor of light.

READ ROMANS 13

Prayer: Lord, may I lay aside the deeds of darkness and put on the armor of light. I want to put on the Lord Jesus Christ and make no provision for the flesh in regard to its lusts.

Meditation passage for today: verses 8, 10, 12-14

Day 273—Romans 14

One of the purposes of this epistle was to encourage the Jews and Gentiles in the church in Rome to develop a spirit of unity in one body. To this end, Paul outlined the principles and practice of Christian liberty as this relates to different levels of spiritual maturity. Concerning matters of conscience rather than command, those who cannot indulge should not judge those who can, and those who can indulge should not look down on those who cannot. At the same time, those who have faith in these areas should voluntarily restrict themselves when in the presence of those who do not, so they will not cause the latter to stumble. In all things we are to "pursue the things which make for peace and the building up of one another."

READ ROMANS 14

Prayer: *Lord, thank you for this reminder that the kingdom of God is not eating and drinking but righteousness, peace, and joy in the Holy Spirit.*

Meditation passage for today: verses 7–10, 17, 19, 22

Day 274—Romans 15

W hen Paul wrote this epistle, he wanted to prepare the Christians in Rome for his planned visit to them (which was delayed by his two-year imprisonment in Caesarea) and to ground them in the knowledge of the faith. Paul also wanted to solicit the prayer support of these believers in the Imperial City at a transitional point in his ministry. He had completed his apostolic task of laying the foundation for the gospel in the eastern provinces and was now hoping to do the same in the western provinces.

Paul informed his Roman readers, some of whom he had already met in his travels (16:1-15), of his intention to visit them after he completed his mission of delivering a collection from the churches of Macedonia and Achaia to the poor among the saints in Jerusalem (15:20-29).

READ ROMANS 15

Prayer: *God of hope, fill me with all joy and peace in believing, so that I will abound in hope by the power of the Holy Spirit.*

Meditation passage for today: verses 1-7, 13

Day 275—1 Corinthians 1

First Corinthians is a very practical treatise on the application of Christian principles to a wide variety of personal and corporate issues. The book includes the need for unity in the body of believers, church discipline for sexual immorality, counsel concerning marriage, and liberty regarding doubtful things. Other practical issues addressed include the problem of litigation between believers, guidelines for public worship and the use of spiritual gifts, and the nature of the resurrection.

Paul's first concern in this letter is the problem of false pride and divisiveness caused by focusing on people rather than the Lord (1:1–17). Human wisdom is totally inadequate; only the power and wisdom of God can bring salvation (1:18–31).

READ 1 CORINTHIANS 1

Prayer: *Lord, it is by your doing that we are in Christ Jesus, who became to us wisdom from God, righteousness, sanctification, and redemption. May I boast only in you.*

Meditation passage for today: verses 10, 18, 21–31

Day 276—1 Corinthians 2

Corinth was a thriving center of commerce, with two seaports strategically located on a narrow isthmus between the Aegean and the Adriatic Seas. This city was also a center of idolatry and immorality, where pleasure seekers would come to be entertained. During his second missionary journey, Paul established a church in this corrupt city, and he taught the Scriptures there for eighteen months in A.D. 51–52. Paul wrote this epistle to the church at Corinth (5:9 indicates that he had written at least one previous letter to them) in A.D. 56, during his third missionary journey near the end of his years of ministry in the city of Ephesus (16:5–8).

In chapter 2 Paul argues that the gospel transcends human wisdom and must be spiritually discerned, since it cannot be grasped by the natural mind.

READ 1 CORINTHIANS 2

Prayer: *Lord, thank you for your indwelling Spirit, who leads me to know the truth about Jesus, the Lord of glory. I rest my faith not on the wisdom of men but on the power of God.*

Meditation passage for today: verses 5, 9, 14–16

Day 277—1 Corinthians 3

The church at Corinth was plagued by an immature and divisive spirit, as various members oriented themselves around human personalities rather than the Person and work of Christ. Paul therefore exhorts them to focus on the Lord rather than the Lord's servants.

Using an agricultural metaphor, Paul said that it is God who causes growth. Switching to an architectural metaphor, the apostle argued that Jesus Christ is the foundation upon which we must build. As we build on this foundation, we will be rewarded for that which endures on the day when God tests the quality of our work. Since the Holy Spirit dwells in us, we should walk in the wisdom of looking to Jesus rather than being impressed by people.

READ 1 CORINTHIANS 3

Prayer: *Lord, may I find my identity, dignity, and worth in Christ Jesus rather than in the superficial things that may impress people but are passing away.*

Meditation passage for today: verses 6–7, 11–17, 21–23

Day 278—1 Corinthians 6

Having dealt with the problem of factions in the church (1:1–4:21), Paul turned to the problem of incest between a member of the church and his stepmother. He exhorted the church to exercise corporate discipline by removing the offender from their fellowship until he repented (5:1–13). The third problem was that of litigation between believers, and Paul instructed them to settle their differences among themselves without resorting to the civil courts (6:1–8). The fourth problem Paul addressed in this epistle is that of sexual immorality (6:9–20). He argued that since the believer's body is a temple of the Holy Spirit, we must flee immorality and glorify God in our bodies.

READ 1 CORINTHIANS 6

Prayer: *Lord, I give thanks that I was washed, sanctified, and justified in the name of the Lord Jesus Christ and in the Spirit of my God. Since I have been bought with a price, I want to glorify you in my body.*

Meditation passage for today: verses 2, 11–12, 19–20

Day 279—1 Corinthians 7

In chapters 7–16, Paul discusses specific questions that had been raised and offers spiritual perspectives on four areas. The first of these areas includes the issues of marriage, celibacy, divorce, and remarriage. Each of these is addressed in chapter 7.

The apostle affirms the place of marriage in the economy of God but at the same time teaches that those who have the gift of celibacy would do better not to marry in order that they may be focused on the things of the Lord. Those who are married do not have authority over their own bodies but should seek to please their spouse. Those who are called to remain unmarried have the advantage of "undistracted devotion to the Lord," which Paul regarded as an advantage in view of Christ's imminent return.

READ 1 CORINTHIANS 7

Prayer: *Lord, you distribute your gifts and callings in ways that are uniquely appropriate to each of your people. May I seek to please you and to be faithful to your calling in my life.*

Meditation passage for today: verses 4, 7, 17, 29–31

Day 280—1 Corinthians 8

The second problem Paul discussed is eating food offered to idols, reminding us of the importance of doing all things to the glory of God as well as the edification of others (8:1–11:1). The apostle stated that those who knew that there is but one God and that idols are meaningless were at liberty to partake of food that had been offered in the pagan temples. However, he warned these Christians not to allow their liberty to become a stumbling block for those who did not have this knowledge.

Knowledge can make one arrogant if it is not tempered by the love of Christ, which seeks to nurture other people. Thus, it is better not to exercise one's freedom in cases where this would cause another's conscience to be wounded.

READ 1 CORINTHIANS 8

Prayer: *Lord, I acknowledge that there is but one God, the Father, from whom all things come; I exist for him. There is one Lord, Jesus Christ, by whom all things were created; I exist through him.*

Meditation passage for today: verses 1–3, 6

Day 281–1 Corinthians 9

Paul used his own life to illustrate the twin principles of liberty in Christ and the law of love. As an apostle, he had a right to receive his living from the ministry of the Word, but to prevent the Corinthians from stumbling over the issue of his "charging" for the gospel, Paul chose to work for his living while he was in their midst. As he argued in Romans 14, believers must sometimes limit their liberty for the sake of those whose faith is weaker.

Paul did everything for the sake of the gospel, including adapting himself to varying circumstances in order to gain common ground without compromise. Although he understood his liberty, he disciplined himself so that he would not be disqualified from being rewarded at the end of his race.

READ 1 CORINTHIANS 9

Prayer: *Lord, as I grow in the understanding of my true freedom in Christ, may I also consider the needs of others and limit my liberty, when necessary, to display the love of Jesus to them.*

Meditation passage for today: verses 19–23

Day 282—1 Corinthians 13

The third problem Paul addressed relates to public worship, including improper observance of the Lord's Supper and the selfish use of spiritual gifts (11:2–14:40). The apostle taught that the body of Christ is a unity within diversity, and that the multiplicity of spiritual gifts must be exercised in love for the edification of the whole body.

This great chapter on love is sandwiched right in the middle of Paul's teaching concerning the use and abuse of spiritual gifts. Even the most dramatic gifts and sacrificial deeds are useless and dead if they are not animated by God's love. All these gifts will not endure when we see the Lord face-to-face, but love will abide.

READ 1 CORINTHIANS 13

Prayer: *Lord, the love that comes from you is patient, kind, and not jealous; it does not brag and is not arrogant, does not act unbecomingly; it does not seek its own, is not provoked, does not take into account a wrong suffered, does not rejoice in unrighteousness, but rejoices with the truth; it bears all things, believes all things, hopes all things, endures all things. Grant your love to work through me.*

Meditation passage for today: verses 4–7, 13

Day 283—1 Corinthians 15

The fourth problem Paul discussed concerns misunder-standings about the Resurrection. Paul's historical and theological defense of the Resurrection includes teaching on the nature of the resurrected body. The Corinthians evidently had been struggling over this issue; the Greeks disdained the idea of a resurrected body. Paul recounted the post–Resurrection appearances of Jesus and argued that if there is no resurrec-tion of the dead, Christ has not been raised and we are still in our sins. But since he has been raised, he has abolished death and has assured us that our perishable and natural bodies will be raised as imperishable and spiritual bodies. We live in the hope that our toil is not in vain in the Lord because one day this mortal will put on immortality.

READ 1 CORINTHIANS 15

Prayer: *Lord, I rejoice in the hope of the resurrected, glorious, imperish-able, spiritual, heavenly immortality that you promise to all who have entrusted themselves to your resurrected Son.*

Meditation passage for today: verses 3–4, 20–22, 42–44, 51–54, 58

Day 284—2 Corinthians 1

Second Corinthians is an intensely personal epistle that reveals the heart of the apostle Paul, his motives for ministry, and how he conducted himself in the service of others. His defense of the integrity of his ministry with the Corinthians in the face of attacks and wrongful allegations by false teachers gives us a model for the way we should pursue integrity. If we follow Paul's example when we are impugned, we will have a clear conscience before God and a faithful record before people.

Although the majority of believers in Corinth repented of their opposition to Paul's apostolic authority, there was still an unrepentant minority, evidently led by a group of Judaizers (chapters 10–13), who continued to challenge him. Paul wrote this epistle to defend his conduct, character, and apostolic calling. This is the primary theme that ties this letter together, even in the portion that was addressed to the repentant majority (chapters 1–9).

READ 2 CORINTHIANS 1

Prayer: *Lord, you are the Father of mercies and God of all comfort. I thank you for comforting me in my affliction so that I will be able to comfort others also.*

Meditation passage for today: verses 3–4, 21–22

Day 285—2 Corinthians 4

Paul began this epistle with thanksgiving for God's comfort in his hardships (1:1–11). He then explained that his
delay in visiting the Corinthians was not due to wavering,
but it was to give them sufficient time to repent (1:12–2:4). He
asked them to restore the repentant offender (2:5–13) and
went on to defend the conduct, content, and motivation of
his ministry among them (2:14–6:10). After an exhortation to
be separate from defilement (6:11–7:1), Paul described the
encouragement he received from Titus' report (7:2–16).

In spite of the many adversities he encountered, Paul did
not lose heart, because he had developed an eternal perspective on temporal affliction. As he wrote in Romans 8:18, "I
consider that the sufferings of this present time are not worthy to be compared with the glory that is to be revealed to
us."

READ 2 CORINTHIANS 4

Prayer: *Lord, thank you that momentary, light affliction is producing
for me an eternal weight of glory far beyond all comparison. May I set
my heart on the things which are not seen.*

Meditation passage for today: verses 6–7, 16–18

Day 286—2 Corinthians 5

This important chapter reveals important truths concerning the resurrection and judgment of believers (5:1–10) and the meaning and ministry of reconciliation (5:11–21). Although "there is now no condemnation for those who are in Christ Jesus" (Rom 8:1), believers will still appear before the judgment seat of Christ to be rewarded according to their works. It is wise to remember the brevity of our temporal sojourn so that we will invest our earthly time wisely before we are at home with the Lord. We have been called to a ministry of reconciliation in our spheres of influence as ambassadors for Christ. When we leave this planet, we will never again have the opportunity of sharing the gospel or serving the needy.

READ 2 CORINTHIANS 5

Prayer: *Lord, you made Jesus who knew no sin to be sin on our behalf, so that we might become the righteousness of God in him.*

Meditation passage for today: verses 6–10, 14–17, 21

Day 287—2 Corinthians 8

The apostle appealed to the Corinthians to follow the Macedonians' example of generosity by keeping their promise of contributing to the collection he was planning to bring to the believers in Judea (chapters 8–9). These two chapters develop the central New Testament teaching on financial stewardship and illustrate a number of timeless principles.

Just as the believers in Macedonia gave with a sense of joyful participation in spite of their meager resources, so Paul encouraged the Corinthians to be participants in the gracious work of God in contributing to the needs of others. When we give ourselves first to the Lord (verse 5), then we are empowered to give ourselves to others by the will of God.

READ 2 CORINTHIANS 8

Prayer: *Lord, I glory in the grace of our Lord Jesus Christ, that though he was rich, yet for our sake he became poor, so that we through his poverty might become rich.*

Meditation passage for today: verses 3, 5, 9, 14, 21

Day 288—2 Corinthians 9

Pointing to the example of the Macedonians, who liberally gave to the needy brethren in Jerusalem (8:1–6), Paul appealed to the Corinthians to keep their promise by doing the same (8:7–9:15). In this connection, Paul commended the messengers he had sent to Corinth to make arrangements for the large gift they had promised. The apostle assured them that their generosity would be more than amply rewarded by God.

Paul urges his readers not only to be bountiful in their giving but to give out of a cheerful rather than grudging heart. In the same way, God is able to make all grace abound to them and to make them sufficient in everything.

READ 2 CORINTHIANS 9

Prayer: *Lord, you are able to make all grace abound to me, so that always having all sufficiency in everything, I may have an abundance for every good deed. Thanks be to you for your indescribable gift!*

Meditation passage for today: verses 6–8, 15

Day 289—2 Corinthians 12

Turning his attention to the unrepentant minority who continued to challenge his authority, Paul defended his apostolic calling and credentials (chapters 10–13). His meekness in their presence did not minimize his authority (chapter 10), and though he was loath to boast about them, his knowledge, honesty, achievements, persecutions, visions, and miraculous signs all vindicated his apostolic claims (11–12:13). He concluded by telling of his plans for a third visit and warned them to repent before he came (12:14–13:14).

Paul's vision of being caught up into paradise led to his thorn in the flesh as God's means of keeping him weak, so that he could minister out of Christ's power rather than his own.

READ 2 CORINTHIANS 12

Prayer: *Lord, your grace is sufficient for me, for power is perfected in weakness. May I walk and serve through dependence on your power rather than my own resources.*

Meditation passage for today: verses 9–10, 19

Day 290—Galatians 5

The gospel of grace (as opposed to the trap of works-based religiosity) finds its clearest exposition in the epistle to the Galatians. There is a natural human tendency to suppose that we can or must earn God's approval, acceptance, love, or forgiveness through our own effort and achievement.

It is not uncommon, even for those who understand that salvation is a gift of God's grace through faith in Christ Jesus, to slip into the error of thinking that spiritual growth is primarily a matter of human effort and merit. Galatians corrects this error by stressing that the same principle that brings about our justification (grace through faith) also brings about our sanctification. When we walk by the Spirit, we are empowered to bear the spiritual fruit of love, joy, peace, patience, kindness, goodness, faithfulness, gentleness, and self-control.

READ GALATIANS 5

Prayer: *Lord, may I walk in the power of your Holy Spirit by abiding in Christ Jesus. I desire to display the fruit of the Spirit rather than the deeds of the flesh.*

Meditation passage for today: verses 5, 13–14, 16, 22–25

Day 291—Galatians 6

Paul began this epistle with a biographical argument (chapters 1-2) that affirmed the divine origin of his apostleship and his message of the gospel of grace in contrast to the distortion of the gospel by false teachers. He recounted how God gave him the message of justification by faith in Christ, and how this was confirmed by the apostles. Paul then developed a theological argument (chapters 3-4) in defense of justification by faith. He contended that the law was given not to save people but to bring them to faith. The apostle concluded with a moral argument (chapters 5-6) that anticipates the objection that the liberty of grace could degenerate into license and lawlessness. Paul insisted that faith expressing itself through love and empowered by the Holy Spirit will overcome the propensities of the flesh and fulfill the requirements of the law.

READ GALATIANS 6

Prayer: *Lord, may I never boast except in the cross of our Lord Jesus Christ, through which the world has been crucified to me, and I to the world.*

Meditation passage for today: verses 2, 7-10, 14

Day 292—Ephesians 1

Most believers have only a vague notion of their true identity and spiritual wealth. As a consequence, they live like spiritual paupers without appropriating the marvelous resources that God has placed at their disposal. They are frustrated when they hear messages that tell them how they ought to order their lives, because they do not know how to accomplish this, and when they try, they do not succeed.

The first half of Ephesians (chapters 1–3) offers a solution to this dilemma by exposing us to the treasury of spiritual blessings that are already ours in Christ if we will lay hold of them by faith in his promises. By looking to him for our identity and empowerment, we discover that it is possible through his grace to fulfill the commands that are developed in the second half of Ephesians (chapters 4–6).

READ EPHESIANS 1

Prayer: *Lord, I pray that you will give me a spirit of wisdom and of revelation in the true knowledge of our Lord Jesus Christ.*

Meditation passage for today: verses 3–14, 17–19

Day 293—Ephesians 2

Our position in Christ (chapters 1–3) lays the foundation for our practice in Christ (chapters 4–6). After a prologue, Paul praised the triune God for the work of the Father in choosing us (1:3–6), the Son in redeeming us (1:7–12), and the Spirit for sealing us (1:13–14). This marvelous hymn to God's grace is followed by a prayer for spiritual illumination in the knowledge of our calling, inheritance, and power (1:15–23). Paul contrasted his readers' former spiritual condition without Christ with the life and hope that salvation by grace through faith has given them (2:1–10). This redemption includes Jews yet also extends to Gentiles, who previously were "strangers to the covenants of promise." In Christ, the two for the first time have become "fellow citizens with the saints" and members of one body (2:11–22).

READ EPHESIANS 2

Prayer: *Lord, thank you that it is by grace that we have been saved through faith; and that not of ourselves. Grace is the gift of God; not as a result of works, so that no one may boast.*

Meditation passage for today: verses 4–10

Day 294—Ephesians 3

Ephesians as a whole, and especially the first three chapters, is full of rich imagery and thought, and it develops insights about the believer's position in Christ that are both profound and powerful. The two prayers in this book (1:15–23; 3:14–21) are among the most significant in the Bible, and they can be used with great profit. The unification of Jew and Gentile in one body was formerly a mystery that has now become manifest (3:1–13). In his second prayer, Paul asked that his readers be strengthened with God's power and with the knowledge of the love of Christ (3:14–21).

Paul wrote this epistle to encourage his readers to grow into spiritual maturity by laying hold of the resources they have in Christ. These resources are for building each other up through the use of spiritual gifts and through serving one another out of Christ's love.

READ EPHESIANS 3

Prayer: *Lord, strengthen me with power through your indwelling Spirit so that Christ may dwell in my heart through faith, and that I would be rooted and grounded in his love.*

Meditation passage for today: verses 16–21

Day 295—Ephesians 4

Paul's theme in Ephesians is captured in the pivotal verse that links the two major sections together: "Therefore I, the prisoner of the Lord, implore you to walk in a manner worthy of the calling with which you have been called" (4:1). This remarkable chapter about the unity and diversity of the body of Christ marks the application of the glorious truths about our true position in Christ in Ephesians 1–3. Paul's passion was that people would not only understand who they are in their vertical relationship with Christ but also express this new identity in their horizontal relationships with one another. The gifts of the Holy Spirit were given to empower us to serve other members of the body in such a way that we build each other up and grow together in ever greater maturity and Christlike character. By "speaking the truth in love" we encourage and equip others to "grow up in all aspects into him."

READ EPHESIANS 4

Prayer: *Lord, I want to be renewed in the spirit of my mind and put on the righteousness and true holiness of the new creation I have become in Christ. Please empower me to love and serve others in such a way that they will be built up and encouraged in him.*

Meditation passage for today: verses 4–7, 15, 22–24, 32

Day 296—Ephesians 5

In the second half of Ephesians, Paul turned from the privileges of the believer to the responsibilities of the believer. He exhorted his readers to grow in unity and in maturity through the loving exercise of their spiritual gifts (4:1–16). He called them to walk in the power of the new self and to practice righteousness, truth, self-control, and forgiveness (4:17–32).

As God's beloved children, we are also to live in the light and avoid the deeds of darkness (5:1–21). All our relationships—as wives and husbands (5:22–33), children and parents (6:1–4), and slaves and masters (6:5–9)—are to be transformed by the love of Christ. Paul admonished us to stand firm in the spiritual warfare and use the weapons of truth, righteousness, peace, faith, salvation, the Word of God, and prayer (6:10–20).

READ EPHESIANS 5

Prayer: *Lord, I want to imitate you as your beloved child and walk in love, just as Christ also loved me and gave himself up for me, an offering and a sacrifice to God as a fragrant aroma.*

Meditation passage for today: verses 1–2, 8–9, 15–21

Day 297—Ephesians 6

Paul's important expression "in Christ" and its equivalent ("in him") appears in Ephesians thirty-five times, more than in any other New Testament book. The "in Christ" relationship that is available to every believer is rich and multifaceted:

- we have received every spiritual blessing in Christ (1:3);
- we were chosen in Christ (1:4, 11);
- we were adopted as God's children in Christ (1:5);
- we have redemption in Christ (1:7);
- our hope is in Christ (1:12);
- we were sealed in Christ (1:13);
- we were made alive in Christ (2:5);
- we were raised up with Christ and seated with him in the heavenly realms (2:6);
- we are God's workmanship, created in Christ Jesus to do good works (2:10);
- we are joined together in Christ (2:21);
- we are sharers together in the promise in Christ Jesus (3:6);
- we can approach God with freedom and confidence in Christ (3:12); and
- we are called to strengthen ourselves in Christ's mighty power (6:10).

READ EPHESIANS 6

Prayer: *Lord, may I live in dependence upon your strength and put on the full armor of God, so that I will be able to stand firm against the schemes of the devil.*

Meditation passage for today: verses 10–13

Day 298—Philippians 1

Philippians is an epistle of joy and encouragement that inspires its readers to focus their thoughts and actions on the pursuit of Christ. When our joy is threatened by adverse circumstances (chapter 1), disunity among people (chapter 2), the quest for accomplishments (chapter 3), or anxiety (chapter 4), this letter is a powerful tool that can help us get our eyes back on Jesus. Only by pursuing Jesus first will we discover the peace and contentment that comes from God.

Paul began this epistle with a word of thanksgiving for the Philippians and a prayer for their spiritual growth in love and discernment (1:1–11). He then told them about his imprisonment, the progress of the gospel, and his openness to either outcome (exoneration or execution) in his trial (1:12–26). This chapter concludes with an exhortation to contend for the gospel in the face of persecution (1:27–30).

READ PHILIPPIANS 1

Prayer: *Lord, may my love abound more and more in real knowledge and all discernment, so that I may approve the things that are excellent in order to be sincere and blameless until the day of Christ.*

Meditation passage for today: verses 6, 9–11, 21

Day 299—Philippians 2

Paul exhorted his readers in Philippi to maintain a spirit of love and unity by pursuing the mind of Christ Jesus, who served others through his Incarnation and death (2:1–11). He called them to cultivate this attitude (2:12–18) and illustrated it through the sacrificial service of Timothy and Epaphroditus (2:19–30).

While Philippians contains little doctrinal teaching, Paul's use of Christ's self–emptying in 2:5–11 as a model of other–centered humility is one of the most significant passages on the Person and work of Christ in the Bible. This is known as the *kenosis* passage, from the Greek word that speaks of the emptying that was involved in the Incarnation. Christ did not empty himself of his deity but divested himself of the full manifestation of his divine rights and attributes during his earthly life.

READ PHILIPPIANS 2

Prayer: *Lord, may I do nothing from selfishness or empty conceit, but with humility of mind may I regard others as more important than myself. May I have the attitude of Christ Jesus and look out for the interests of others.*

Meditation passage for today: verses 3–13

Day 300—Philippians 3

Turning to the problem of legalistic influences, Paul used the futility of works–based righteousness (3:1–9). Having found true righteousness through faith in Christ, he pressed on toward the goal of the upward call of God in Christ Jesus (3:10–16). He warned about those who set their mind on earthly things and contrasted this with his passion for heavenly things (3:17–21).

Due to its informality, Philippians does not follow an outline but quickly moves through a variety of topics. The words *joy* and *rejoice* appear sixteen times; these words capture the spirit of this epistle. Paul revealed the secrets of being content in every situation (4:12): a single–minded pursuit of the personal knowledge of Christ (3:10) and an understanding that to live is Christ and to die is gain (1:21).

READ PHILIPPIANS 3

Prayer: *Lord, I lay hold of the righteousness that comes through faith in Christ Jesus. May I know him and the power of his resurrection and the fellowship of his sufferings.*

Meditation passage for today: verses 3, 8–14, 20–21

Day 301—Philippians 4

In the last chapter, Paul exhorted the believers in Philippi to maintain unity, to enjoy God's peace by offering all anxieties to God in prayer, and to be content in their circumstances (4:1–13). After thanking them for participating in his ministry though their support, he closed with greetings and a benediction (4:14–23).

Paul wrote this letter to thank the Philippians for their gift, to convey his warm affection for them, and to encourage them to "[stand] firm in one spirit, with one mind striving together for the faith of the gospel" (1:27). He argued that joy springs out of unity and that unity springs out of humility; the ultimate example of humility is the obedience of Christ Jesus to his Father's will (2:5–11).

READ PHILIPPIANS 4

Prayer: *Lord, may I be anxious for nothing, but in everything by prayer and supplication with thanksgiving, may I make my requests known to you. May your peace, which surpasses all comprehension, guard my heart and mind in Christ Jesus.*

Meditation passage for today: verses 4–9, 13, 19

Day 302—Colossians 1

Colossians may be the most Christ-centered book in Scripture—everything in it lifts the mind and heart to "the things above, where Christ is, seated at the right hand of God" (3:1). This epistle edifies the mind as it portrays the supremacy and Person of Christ, and it edifies the heart as it encourages us to pursue him in our conduct and character.

After a brief greeting, Paul thanked God for the Colossians (1:3-8) and prayed that they would come to a deeper knowledge and growth in Christ (1:9-14). He developed his theme of the supremacy of Jesus Christ by demonstrating Christ's preeminence in the realms of creation (1:15-18) and redemption (1:19-2:3).

READ COLOSSIANS 1

Prayer: *Lord, I want to be filled with the knowledge of your will in all spiritual wisdom and understanding, so that I will walk in a manner worthy of you. May I please you in all respects, bearing fruit in every good work and increasing in the knowledge of God.*

Meditation passage for today: verses 9-20

Day 303—Colossians 2

Having presented the preeminence of Christ in creation and redemption, Paul went on to refute the false teachings of those who were promoting deceptive philosophy, legalistic regulations, misguided mysticism, and vain asceticism (2:4–23).

Paul wrote this Christ-centered epistle to combat the erroneous teachings that were beginning to take hold in Colossae, knowing that the best way to refute error is to focus on the truth. He argued that Christ alone is sufficient for all things, and that the ascetic regulations, hidden knowledge, and mystical visions that were being promoted by the false teachers in Colossae were not only inadequate but heretical. Christ holds all the treasures of wisdom and knowledge (2:3), and it is unnecessary to turn to spurious sources to find what he alone can offer.

READ COLOSSIANS 2

Prayer: *Lord, all the treasures of wisdom and knowledge are hidden in Christ, and in him all the fullness of Deity dwells in bodily form. Just as I have received him by faith, so may I walk in him.*

Meditation passage for today: verses 3, 6–10, 13–14

Day 304—Colossians 3

The first half of Colossians presents the person, character, and supremacy of Christ, and the second half explains the believer's pursuit of Christ through submission to him and godly conduct in each area of life. Since we are united with Christ (3:1–4), we are to put the sinful manifestations of the old self to death (3:5–11) and demonstrate the life of the new self in Christ (3:12–17). This inward transformation should be expressed in the transformation of outward relationships in the family, in the marketplace, and in proclamation to unbelievers (3:18–4:6).

Paul urged his readers to keep their hope fixed on Christ alone. As they grow in this hope, it will be manifested in a quality of holiness in their relationships with others that is not based on rules and regulations but on a growing personal relationship with Christ Jesus.

READ COLOSSIANS 3

Prayer: *Lord, when Christ, who is my life, is revealed, then I also will be revealed with him in glory. Whatever I do in word or deed, may I do in the name of the Lord Jesus, giving thanks through him to you.*

Meditation passage for today: verses 1–4, 9–17

Day 305—Colossians 4

Christ is the image of the invisible God by whom and for whom all things were created (1:15–16). In him, all the fullness of the Deity dwells in bodily form (1:15, 19; 2:9), and he sustains the entire cosmos (1:16–17).

Paul redefines the terms used by the Colossian heretics by arguing that only in Christ can one discover the true *gnosis* (knowledge) and *pleroma* (fullness). In him are hidden "all the treasures of wisdom and knowledge" (2:3). He is the source of redemption and reconciliation to God (1:14, 20–22; 2:11–15), and he is the all-sufficient Savior of those who know him (1:28; 2:10; 3:1–4). Christ is the "head of the body, the church; and he is the beginning, the firstborn from the dead, so that he himself will come to have first place in everything" (1:18).

READ COLOSSIANS 4

Prayer: *Lord, may I conduct myself with wisdom toward those who do not know Christ, making the most of the opportunity. May my speech always be with grace, so that I will know how I should respond to each person.*

Meditation passage for today: verses 2–6

Day 306—1 Thessalonians 1

This warm and personal epistle encourages us to remain steadfast in our faith and to grow in sanctification. It gives us a model for relational ministry as Paul describes the way he worked with and nurtured the Thessalonians. It exemplifies the kind of personal concern we should adopt for those we have been privileged to serve. This letter also contains critical insights on the coming of the Lord for his saints and the nature of "the Day of the Lord."

Paul began this epistle of personal reflection, exhortation, encouragement, and instruction by giving thanks for the report he had received from Timothy about their work produced by faith, their labor prompted by love, and their endurance inspired by hope in Christ (1:1–3). He rejoiced that their faith had inspired all the believers in Macedonia and Achaia (1:4–10).

READ 1 THESSALONIANS 1

Prayer: *Lord, you have called me to serve you, the living and true God, and to wait for your Son from heaven. Thank you that you raised him from the dead, and he will rescue us from the wrath to come.*

Meditation passage for today: verses 3–5, 9–10

Day 307—1 Thessalonians 2

Paul's word of thanksgiving for the Thessalonians is followed by a review of his ministry in their midst and a defense of his care, concern, motives, and message (2:1-16).

First Thessalonians centers on the theme of the salvation and spiritual growth of the believers in Thessalonica. After hearing Timothy's report about the steadfastness of the Thessalonians' faith, Paul wrote this epistle to tell them how thankful he was for the reality of their growing faith and love in the face of persecution. He also responded to the false accusations of the Jewish opposition by reminding his readers of the selfless way he ministered to them and the truthfulness of the message he imparted to them.

READ 1 THESSALONIANS 2

Prayer: *Lord, may I love and serve others out of tenderness and affection as I encourage them to walk in a manner worthy of the God who calls us to his own kingdom and glory.*

Meditation passage for today: verses 7–8, 13, 19–20

Day 308—1 Thessalonians 3

Paul explained that he was concerned after his departure from the Thessalonians about their spiritual condition, and he expressed his profound encouragement to hear that their faith and love were continuing to grow (2:17–3:10). Before moving on to a series of exhortations and instructions, Paul paused to pray for their continued spiritual progress (3:11–13).

This personal letter has much in common with 2 Corinthians; in both letters Paul defended his message and character in view of slanderous opposition. In his defense of his ministry, Paul revealed his motives, his compassion, his dedication, his tenderness, and his concern for the people God had called him to serve.

READ 1 THESSALONIANS 3

Prayer: *Lord, cause your children to increase and abound in our love for one another, so that you may establish our hearts without blame in holiness before you.*

Meditation passage for today: verses 9–13

Day 309—1 Thessalonians 4

Paul's practical exhortations begin with a reminder of his teaching on sexual purity, brotherly love, and personal responsibility (4:1–12). In answer to their concern about the destiny of believers who have died in Christ, the apostle comforted them with the hope of resurrection and reunion in Christ at his coming (4:13–18).

Christ is seen in this epistle as the Lord who will return from heaven and rescue his people from the coming wrath (1:10; 5:4–11). The certainty of his coming is a great source of hope for those who trust in him, because both the dead in Christ and those who are alive when he comes will be resurrected and united in him (4:13–18). He will sanctify (3:13; 5:23) and reward (2:19–20) all who hope in him.

READ 1 THESSALONIANS 4

Prayer: *Lord, thank you for the blessed hope of being caught up to meet the Lord Jesus in the air when he descends from heaven to receive us to himself.*

Meditation passage for today: verses 13–18

Day 310—1 Thessalonians 5

Paul continued with a discourse on the future Day of the Lord and exhorted the Thessalonians to be alert and self-controlled, as children of the light whose destiny is to live together with Christ (5:1–11). The epistle ends with specific admonitions and instructions that relate to their sanctification (5:12–22) and with a benediction and parting thoughts (5:23–28).

Both of Paul's Thessalonian epistles deal with matters of eschatology (prophecy), and all five chapters of First Thessalonians refer to the return of Christ (1:10; 2:19; 3:13; 4:13–18; 5:1–11, 23). The prophetic material in 4:13–5:11 is very vivid and practical, and this is one of the most important biblical passages concerning the coming of Christ.

READ 1 THESSALONIANS 5

Prayer: *Lord, may I rejoice always, pray without ceasing, and in everything give thanks; for this is your will for me in Christ Jesus.*

Meditation passage for today: verses 8–11, 16–18, 23

Day 311—2 Thessalonians 1

The truth of Paul's teaching in his first epistle to the Thessalonians was distorted by false teachers, who claimed that the Day of the Lord was already taking place, and this led in turn to a mentality of passivity and idleness. This corrective epistle is of great value in clarifying the biblical teaching concerning the coming Day of the Lord as well as promoting a balance between waiting and working.

This letter begins with a salutation (1:1-2) and a word of thanksgiving for the growing faith and perseverance of the believers in Thessalonica in the face of mounting opposition (1:3-4). Paul encouraged them to endure, knowing that their sufferings would be repaid and that God would deal in righteousness with those who had been oppressing them (1:5-10). The first chapter ends with a prayer that God will fulfill his good purposes in their lives (1:11-13).

READ 2 THESSALONIANS 1

Prayer: *Lord, count me worthy of your calling, and fulfill every desire for goodness and the work of faith with power, so that the name of the Lord Jesus will be glorified.*

Meditation passage for today: verses 11–12

Day 312—2 Thessalonians 2

In view of some prophecy or a report falsely attributed to Paul, the church was being disturbed by the deception that the Day of the Lord (see 1 Thes 5:1–11) had come. Paul showed that this could not be so until the man of lawlessness was revealed and the one who held him back was taken out of the way (2:1–12). Paul added a word of encouragement, exhorted his readers to stand firm, and prayed for them (2:13–17).

The first two chapters of 2 Thessalonians focus on the return of Christ and teach that when he is "revealed from heaven with his mighty angels in flaming fire," those who do not know God and do not obey the gospel of our Lord Jesus will be judged (1:6–10). However, Christ will not judge the earth until the "apostasy comes first, and the man of lawlessness is revealed" (2:3, 6–12). Thus, Paul's teaching on the second coming is a comfort for believers and a warning to unbelievers.

READ 2 THESSALONIANS 2

Prayer: *Lord, may our Lord Jesus Christ himself and God our Father, who has loved us and given us eternal comfort and good hope by grace, comfort and strengthen our hearts in every good work and word.*

Meditation passage for today: verses 13–14, 16–17

Day 313—2 Thessalonians 3

After a request for prayer on his behalf (3:1-5), Paul admonished those among the Thessalonians who had become idle and were living off the resources of others rather than earning their own provisions (3:6-15). The doctrine of the return of Christ should stimulate responsible living rather than indolence. This brief epistle concludes with a benediction and greetings (3:16-18).

The theme of 2 Thessalonians is comfort and correction in view of practical and doctrinal obstacles to spiritual maturity. Those who followed Jesus in Thessalonica needed to know that their persecution would be vindicated at the return of Christ, that the Day of the Lord was yet in the future, and that they should continue to be diligent rather than undisciplined while they awaited the coming of the Lord.

READ 2 THESSALONIANS 3

Prayer: *Lord, direct my heart into the love of God and into the steadfastness of Christ.*

Meditation passage for today: verses 3, 5, 13

Day 314—1 Timothy 1

First Timothy is full of specific principles of leadership and holy living. It is particularly relevant to anyone who is in a position of spiritual influence. This is an extremely practical book that touches on issues of doctrine, public worship, the problem of false teaching, the treatment of various groups within the church, wealth, contentment, and personal integrity.

Paul began this letter by warning his young associate about the problem of the misuse of the Law of Moses by false teachers (1:3-11). He looked back to his dramatic conversion to Christ and encouraged Timothy to fulfill his own God-ordained purpose by fighting the good fight (1:12-20).

READ 1 TIMOTHY 1

Prayer: *Lord, you are the King eternal, immortal, invisible, the only God; to you be honor and glory forever and ever.*

Meditation passage for today: verses 5, 14-17

Day 315—1 Timothy 2

Turning to matters of church worship and leadership, Paul stressed that the men of the church should be leaders in prayer (2:1–8) and that the women should be characterized by inner godliness (2:9–15).

While First Timothy is a personal letter, it was written in an authoritative and exhortative tone because of the specific problems it addressed in light of Timothy's leadership responsibilities during Paul's absence from Ephesus. Since it was written to his trusted and personal associate, it refers to doctrine without developing it and encourages Timothy to stand firm in the truth. This epistle contains the clearest and most explicit directions for the organization and administration of the church in the Bible.

READ 1 TIMOTHY 2

Prayer: *Lord, I acknowledge that there is one God and one mediator also between God and men, the man Christ Jesus, who gave himself as a ransom for all, the testimony given at the proper time.*

Meditation passage for today: verses 1–6

Day 316—1 Timothy 3

Paul's purpose in writing this epistle to his disciple and emissary, Timothy, is clear in 3:15: "In case I am delayed, I write so that you will know how one ought to conduct himself in the household of God, which is the church of the living God, the pillar and support of the truth." This letter is really a leadership manual that was designed to provide practical guidance to Timothy on a number of specific issues, including personal exhortations to godliness, development of his spiritual gifts, directions for worship in the churches, defending apostolic doctrine in the face of false teaching, instructions about widows and elders, the temptations of wealth, and faithfulness to his calling.

Paul listed the qualifications for overseers in 3:1–7 (in the New Testament church, bishops and elders referred to the same office; see Acts 20:17, 28; Ti 1:5, 7) and the qualifications for deacons in 3:8–13.

READ 1 TIMOTHY 3

Prayer: *Lord, by common confession, great is the mystery of godliness: he who was revealed in the flesh, was vindicated in the Spirit, seen by angels, proclaimed among the nations, believed on in the world, taken up in glory.*

Meditation passage for today: verse 16

Day 317—1 Timothy 4

The epistles of 1 and 2 Timothy and Titus do not fit against the background of the Book of Acts, since they were written after Paul's release from his first Roman imprisonment (see Acts 28). The events in the last years of Paul's life must be reconstructed from clues that are provided in these epistles. It appears that in spite of his statement in Acts 20:25, Paul did return to Ephesus, and after Timothy joined him there, he instructed Timothy to stay in Ephesus while he went into Macedonia (1:3). He wrote this epistle to Timothy while in Macedonia (probably Philippi) in A.D. 62 or 63, when he realized his return to Ephesus might be delayed (3:14-15).

In view of the influence of false teachers, Paul exhorted Timothy to counter error with the truths of the gospel and to set an example to others of purity of life and doctrine as he continued to use his spiritual gift (4:1-16).

READ 1 TIMOTHY 4

Prayer: *Lord, may I hold fast to the truth and discipline myself for the purpose of godliness as I fix my hope on you, the living God.*

Meditation passage for today: verses 4-5

Day 318—1 Timothy 5

Paul's two letters to Timothy and his letter to Titus are collectively known as the pastoral epistles because they deal with issues of shepherding and oversight of local churches. In this chapter, Paul gave his associate Timothy specific instructions on how the church should provide for widows and for the elders who directed the affairs of the church (5:1–25).

First Timothy presents Christ Jesus as the one mediator between God and humanity who gave himself as a ransom for all (2:5–6). Christ Jesus came into the world to save sinners, and he is "the Savior of all men, especially of believers" (1:15; 4:10). It is in him that strength, mercy, faith, love, salvation, hope, godliness, and contentment (1:12–14; 2:3–6; 4:10; 6:6) are to be found.

READ 1 TIMOTHY 5

Prayer: *Lord, may I do nothing in a spirit of partiality. I ask for your power to show love, patience, kindness, and goodness to each person I encounter.*

Meditation passage for today: verses 21, 24–25

Day 319—1 Timothy 6

After a word concerning those who are slaves (6:1-2), Paul condemned the false teaching that godliness is a means to financial gain, affirming instead that contentment is more valuable than material abundance (6:3-10). He concluded this epistle with a charge to Timothy to endure in the good fight of the faith (6:11-16) and with a final word about those who are rich in this present world (6:17-21).

The pastoral epistles are Paul's only recorded letters to individuals (his letter to Philemon was addressed to several people). As the last of Paul's letters in Scripture, 1 Timothy and Titus were written after his first imprisonment, and 2 Timothy was written during his second imprisonment, near the end of his life.

READ 1 TIMOTHY 6

Prayer: *Lord, you are the blessed and only Sovereign, the King of Kings and Lord of Lords, who alone possesses immortality and dwells in unapproachable light, whom no man has seen or can see. To you be honor and eternal dominion!*

Meditation passage for today: verses 6–16

Day 320—2 Timothy 1

Second Timothy contains Paul's parting words to his younger associate, Timothy, and by listening in, we can gain wise and godly counsel that is as relevant to the problems we face today as it was to the problems Timothy faced in the first century. This is a powerful manual for spiritual combat, and it encourages us to be diligent and courageous and to make the most of the opportunities that God has given us.

After a brief greeting, Paul reviewed Timothy's conversion and reminded him to fan into flame the gift he had received, and to overcome timidity with God's power (1:1–7). He invited Timothy to join with him in suffering for the gospel, knowing that Christ would guard whatever he entrusted to him (1:8–14). Paul commended Onesiphorus, who had supported Paul in Rome when other believers had abandoned him (1:15–18).

READ 2 TIMOTHY 1

Prayer: *Lord, I know whom I have believed, and I am convinced that he is able to guard what I have entrusted to him until the day of Christ Jesus.*

Meditation passage for today: verses 7–12

Day 321—2 Timothy 2

Paul encouraged his younger associate Timothy to engage in a ministry of reproducing the life of Christ in others and of equipping them to do the same. He used the metaphors of a soldier, an athlete, and a farmer to convey the need for diligence in discipleship (2:1–13). He admonished Timothy to be strong in the Word of Truth and to avoid god-less chatter, youthful lusts, and fruitless quarrels (2:14–26).

Those who wish to be active and effective in the Lord's service should call on the Lord out of a pure heart. If we pray for the eyes to see what God is doing in our lives, we will realize we have more ministry opportunities than we thought.

READ 2 TIMOTHY 2

Prayer: *Lord, I want to be a vessel for honor, sanctified and useful for the Master, prepared for every good work. By your grace and power, I want to participate in your eternal plan. Open my eyes to the opportunities you give me to love and serve others with eternal values at heart.*

Meditation passage for today: verses 1–2, 10–13, 22

Day 322—2 Timothy 3

Paul predicted a time of increasing arrogance, rebelliousness, and vulnerability to spiritual deception (3:1–9) and warned Timothy that he could expect that persecution for the sake of following Christ would increase (3:10–13). He reminded Timothy to stay strong in Scripture and to use it effectively in this spiritual combat (3:14–17).

Paul's letters to Timothy indicate that the latter was youthful, frequently ill, and timid (see 1 Tm 4:12; 5:23; 2 Tm 1:7), but that he was a trustworthy and gifted teacher. The apostle wrote this letter to encourage him to be faithful to his calling and to stand firm in the face of obstacles to the spread of the gospel. Timothy was encountering a number of hardships, and Paul wanted to strengthen him to handle external persecution and internal problems of false doctrine and dissension within the churches. This was especially urgent in light of the fact that Paul was near-ing the end of his ministry and needed to entrust important areas into the care of his faithful associate and disciple.

READ 2 TIMOTHY 3

Prayer: *Lord, I acknowledge that all Scripture is God-breathed and prof-itable for teaching, for reproof, for correction, for training in righteous-ness, so that we may be adequate, equipped for every good work. Help me to use your Word wisely.*

Meditation passage for today: verses 12, 15–17

Day 323—2 Timothy 4

In his final exhortation, Paul charged his associate to preach and teach the Word, to correct, rebuke, and encourage, and to endure hardship and do the work of an evangelist (4:1–5). Paul concluded this epistle with thoughts about his future reward with Christ and with personal remarks and requests (4:6–22).

As Paul's last recorded epistle (written during his second Roman imprisonment in A.D. 67), 2 Timothy serves as his final testament to the world. He reviewed Christ's faithfulness in his past and commissioned Timothy to carry on the good work of proclaiming Christ in the present. He also looked ahead to the future when he would be rewarded with the crown of righteousness after being brought safely to the Lord's heavenly kingdom.

READ 2 TIMOTHY 4

Prayer: *Lord, by your grace, may I be able to say at the end of my earthly sojourn, "I have fought the good fight, I have finished the course, I have kept the faith."*

Meditation passage for today: verses 1–2, 5, 7–8, 18

Day 324—Titus 1

This epistle is a concise manual of conduct for assemblies of brothers and sisters in Christ. Titus 1 and 1 Timothy 3 are critical to the organization of the local church because they outline God's requirements for the leadership of the body of believers. Titus provides us with instruction on the ordination of elders, dealing with false teachers, the role of different groups within the church, and the relationship between sound doctrine and godly behavior.

Paul's salutation to Titus contains a rich statement of God's redemptive purpose for his people (1:1–4). He then launched into the principal purpose of the letter, which was to provide instructions for the oversight and conduct of the churches in Crete. Paul gave his associate a list of qualifications to assist him in discerning the right people for this leadership office in each church (1:5–9), and then warned him about the problem of corruption and false teaching (1:10–16).

READ TITUS 1

Prayer: *Lord, may I be a servant of your truth and hold fast the faithful word, not only in my thinking but also in my daily practice.*

Meditation passage for today: verses 1–3

Day 325—Titus 2

Paul gave Titus clear directives concerning the way each group (older men, older women, younger women, young men, and slaves) in the assemblies should conduct themselves (2:1–10). This is followed by a concise affirmation of the hope and transforming power of the gospel of Christ (2:11–15).

Titus presents Christ as the supreme manifestation of the grace, mercy, and redemptive purposes of God. It is by his grace that we are justified, and through him we have become heirs who enjoy the hope of eternal life. This hope is in "the appearing of the glory of our great God and Savior, Christ Jesus" (2:13).

READ TITUS 2

Prayer: *Lord, may I deny ungodliness and worldly desires and live sensibly, righteously, and godly in the present age, looking for the blessed hope and the appearing of the glory of our great God and Savior, Christ Jesus.*

Meditation passage for today: verses 11–14

Day 326—Titus 3

A fter an exhortation concerning the general conduct of all
believers (3:1–2), Paul gave a sublime summary of how
the kindness, love, and mercy of God brought about our salvation through grace and not by works (3:3–7). However,
good works should follow from this redemption (3:8). This
letter closes with instructions on dealing with divisive people
(3:9–11) and some final remarks (3:12–15).

Paul wrote this epistle to follow through on his instructions for the appointment of elders in every city in Crete by
giving Titus a list of qualifications to use in this process (1:5–9;
see 1 Tm 3). He emphasized the need for sound doctrine and
illustrated this with three important summaries of the faith
(1:1–3; 2:11–14; 3:3–7).

READ TITUS 3

Prayer: *Lord, you saved us, not on the basis of deeds which we have done
in righteousness but according to your mercy. Thank you for the wash-
ing of regeneration and renewing by the Holy Spirit, whom you poured
out upon us richly through Jesus Christ our Savior, so that being justified by his grace, we would be made heirs according to the hope of eternal life.*

Meditation passage for today: verses 3–7

Day 327—Philemon

Paul's purpose in writing this letter was to appeal to Philemon on behalf of a man who was previously a useless slave, a thief, and a runaway. Because of Onesimus' conversion to faith in Christ, Paul argued that his character had been transformed and that he should be moved from bondage to brotherhood in the eyes of his former master. Just as Philemon himself received grace and forgiveness in Christ, so he must extend the same to this new brother in the Lord. Paul urged Philemon to receive Onesimus just as he would receive him, and he even invited Philemon to charge Onesimus' debt to him.

Philemon is a brief but powerful testimony to the transforming power of faith, forgiveness, and freedom in Christ. This transformation on the vertical level should result in transformation on the horizontal level of our relationships with others. This epistle teaches us that spiritual change produces social change.

READ PHILEMON

Prayer: *Lord, may I no longer view people according to the flesh but according to the way you see them, as people you love and for whom Christ gave his life.*

Meditation passage for today: verses 6, 15–18

Day 328—Hebrews 1

Hebrews is a profound and powerful book that uses a variety of Old Testament passages to present a clear case for the superiority of Christ over everything that preceded him.

Jesus Christ is revealed to be the supreme revelation of God (1:1-3). Since he is worshiped by the angels, he is superior to them (1:4-14). This book of Hebrews adds immeasurably to our understanding of Christ's person and work, and it applies this understanding to the dynamics of spiritual growth in the life of the believer. Hebrews 11 is one of the most extraordinary chapters in Scripture, and it is the clearest exposition of the meaning and rewards of faith in the Bible.

READ HEBREWS 1

Prayer: *Lord, I confess that your Son is the radiance of your glory and the exact representation of your nature, and he upholds all things by the word of his power.*

Meditation passage for today: verses 1–4, 14

Day 329—Hebrews 2

Hebrews contrasts the temporary Aaronic priesthood with Christ as our eternal High Priest in the order of Melchizedek. He is equally divine (1:1-3, 8) and human (2:9, 14, 17-18). He fulfills the three orders of prophet, priest, and king. His perfect and voluntary sacrifice is the fulfillment of all that was anticipated but not realized in the involuntary animal sacrifices of the Old Testament and, unlike those sacrifices, never needs to be repeated. Through his incarnation, Jesus understands the human condition: he became the author of our salvation and our merciful and faithful High Priest. "For since he himself was tempted in that which he has suffered, he is able to come to the aid of those who are tempted."

READ HEBREWS 2

Prayer: *Lord, your Son partook of flesh and blood, that through death he might render powerless him who had the power of death, that is, the devil. Thank you that he frees those who through fear of death were subject to slavery all their lives.*

Meditation passage for today: verses 9-10, 14-18

Day 330—Hebrews 4

The author of Hebrews argued that Jesus is superior to Moses, since Moses was a servant while Christ is the Son (3:1-6). Thus, this book warns of the danger of unbelief and rebellion against him (3:7-19). Christ offers a better rest than Joshua, and this rest is appropriated by faith in him (4:1-13). As our great High Priest in the order of Melchizedek, Christ is able to identify with the human condition because he suffered and "became to all those who obey him the source of eternal salvation" (4:14-5:10).

Since Jesus was tempted in all things as we are, but without sin, he can sympathize with our weaknesses and we can "draw near with confidence to the throne of grace, so that we may receive mercy and find grace to help in time of need."

READ HEBREWS 4

Prayer: *Lord, your Word is living and active and sharper than any two-edged sword, piercing as far as the division of soul and spirit, of both joints and marrow, and able to judge the thoughts and intentions of the heart.*

Meditation passage for today: verses 2, 12-16

Day 331—Hebrews 8

The author urges his readers not to fall away but to press on to spiritual maturity and to put their hope in God's promises (5:11–6:20). Christ's priesthood is superior to that of the Levites (7:1–28), and as such, he is the mediator of a better covenant than the Mosaic covenant (8:1–13).

The author of Hebrews skillfully used a great range of Old Testament quotations and allusions to build a careful case for the finality of Christ's priestly sacrifice. The rich doctrinal contributions of this book include its emphasis on the present priestly ministry of Christ, its development of the atonement of Christ, and its contrasts between the old and new covenants and between the earthly and heavenly sanctuaries. Hebrews sheds a great deal of light on the typology of the Mosaic Law and the offerings and feasts in Leviticus.

READ HEBREWS 8

Prayer: *Lord, I give thanks for Jesus our High Priest, who has taken his seat at the right hand of the throne of the Majesty in the heavens as the mediator of the new covenant.*

Meditation passage for today: verses 1–2, 6

Day 332—Hebrews 9

As our High Priest, Jesus ministers in a better, heavenly tabernacle, and his blood sacrifice is superior to the sacrifices offered in the earthly sanctuary (9:1–10:18).

Hebrews builds a cumulative argument to demonstrate the superiority of Christ over the old covenant, priesthood, and sacrifices. This theme is developed in the frequent use of the word *better* or *superior*, as well as the use of the terms *heavenly* and *perfect* to describe the greatness of Christ's Person and work in comparison to what was previously revealed. He is better than the angels in that they worship him; he is better than Moses in that he created him; he offers a better rest than Joshua, a better priesthood than Levi, a better covenant, a better sanctuary, and a better sacrifice. He also provides the power to live a better life.

READ HEBREWS 9

Prayer: *Lord, it is the blood of Christ, who through the eternal Spirit offered himself without blemish to God, which cleanses my conscience from dead works to serve the living God.*

Meditation passage for today: verses 11–15, 27–28

Day 333—Hebrews 11

Due to the manifold superiority of Christ Jesus, the author of this epistle calls his readers to conduct themselves in obedience to Jesus and to persevere in their sufferings for his sake (10:19–39). Like the obedient men and women of the Old Testament, their faith must be in God's character and their hope must be in his promised heavenly rewards (11:1–40).

Since "faith is the assurance of things hoped for, the conviction of things not seen," we must acknowledge with the men and women who are listed in this chapter that we will not receive the fulfillment of God's promises in this life, but that we await "a better country, that is, a heavenly one."

READ HEBREWS 11

Prayer: *Lord, it is by faith that I understand that the worlds were prepared by your word, so that what is seen was not made out of things that are visible. Without faith it is impossible to please you, for whoever comes to you must believe that you are and that you are a rewarder of those who seek you.*

Meditation passage for today: verses 1, 3, 6, 13, 16, 39–40

Day 334—Hebrews 12

In this chapter, the readers of this epistle are encouraged to endure hardship and discipline for the sake of holiness, and they are warned not to refuse God during these difficult times.

The purpose for the careful exposition in Hebrews of the superiority of Christ's Person, priesthood, covenant, sanctuary, and sacrifice is to show the folly of moving away from the substance back to the shadow. The author sought to exhort his readers not to revert back to Judaism and to encourage them to go on to maturity in Christ. As "strangers and exiles on the earth" (11:13), they must realize that their sufferings for Christ are part of God's purpose, and that their heavenly Father disciplines them for their good, so that they may share his holiness.

READ HEBREWS 12

Prayer: *Lord, may I lay aside every encumbrance and the sin which so easily entangles me, and may I run with endurance the race that is set before me, fixing my eyes on Jesus. He is the author and perfecter of faith, who for the joy set before him endured the cross, despising the shame, and has sat down at the right hand of the throne of God.*

Meditation passage for today: verses 1–3, 11, 22–24, 28–29

Day 335—Hebrews 13

The Letter to the Hebrews concludes with a series of exhortations to purity, contentment, Christlike character, service, and submission (13:1–17), as well as personal instructions and a beautiful benediction (13:18–25).

Hebrews is the only New Testament book whose authorship remains a mystery. Despite its anonymity, its spiritual quality and depth overcame early questions about its inclusion in the New Testament canon. The original readers clearly knew the author (13:18–24), who was an associate of Timothy, but there is no consistent tradition as to his identity. Some in the early church attributed it to Paul, others to Barnabas, to Luke, and to Clement. There are indeed some similarities in the style and content of Hebrews and the Pauline epistles, but there are also enough dissimilarities to lead the majority of New Testament scholars to reject the Pauline authorship theory. Suggestions in modern scholarship include Apollos, Silas (Silvanus), Luke, Philip, and Clement of Rome.

READ HEBREWS 13

Prayer: *Lord, you are the God of peace who brought up from the dead the great Shepherd of the sheep through the blood of the eternal covenant, even Jesus our Lord. May you equip us in every good thing to do your will, working in us that which is pleasing in your sight, through Jesus Christ, to whom be the glory forever and ever.*

Meditation passage for today: verses 1–8, 14–16, 20–21

Day 336—James 1

James is a powerful and practical manual on the application of faith in Christ to the struggles and relationships we encounter every day. With force and clarity, this epistle relates Christlike conduct to a wide range of topics, and it is always convicting to read. James maps the behavior of belief and shows how faith perseveres under trials, resists temptations, responds to Scripture, overcomes favoritism, leads to good works, controls the tongue, produces wisdom, submits to God, resists the lures of the world and the devil, depends on God and not on riches, waits patiently for Christ's coming, and results in answered prayer.

After a brief greeting (1:1) James spoke of the eternal perspective believers need to cultivate when they are facing trials so that they will be able to persevere when tested and tempted (1:2–18). They must not only listen to the Word but apply it to their actions (1:19–27).

READ JAMES 1

Prayer: *Lord, every good and perfect gift is from above, coming down from the Father of lights, with whom there is no variation or shifting shadow.*

Meditation passage for today: verses 2–5, 12, 17–22

Day 337—James 2

Turning to the problem of the preferential treatment of the wealthy, James instructed his readers to love the poor and the rich alike (2:1–13). He contrasted profession of faith with possession of faith and argued that a genuine faith is expressed in deeds (2:14–26). While faith alone justifies us before God (see Rom 4), it is only by the works of faith that we are justified before others (2:24).

James was addressed to "the twelve tribes who are dispersed abroad" (1:1), and this refers to the Hebrew Christians who resided outside of Palestine. These Jewish believers in Jesus the Messiah were encountering many trials, and they needed to be encouraged and exhorted to persevere in their faith. This epistle makes no mention of Gentile believers, and it appears to have been written around A.D. 46–49, before the Jerusalem council in Acts 15. According to Josephus, James was martyred in A.D. 62.

READ JAMES 2

Prayer: *Lord, may I not hold my faith in our glorious Lord Jesus Christ with an attitude of personal favoritism. May my faith in him become evident to others through my works.*

Meditation passage for today: verses 1, 12, 26

Day 338—James 3

The tongue is the hardest thing in nature to control, and our speech can lead to blessing or cursing, to life or to death (3:1–12). James contrasted two kinds of wisdom, the heavenly and the earthly, and exhorted his readers to turn away from envy and selfish ambition to love, mercy, and peace (3:13–18).

This epistle is the primary wisdom literature of the New Testament, and it is strongly influenced by the Book of Proverbs and the Sermon on the Mount. It combines the pithy maxims of the Proverbs with the fiery rhetoric of Amos in its relentlessly ethical stance. It is full of vivid imagery and sharp commands (there are fifty-four imperatives in its 108 verses). This is a very formal letter that differs from the Pauline epistles in that James says nothing at all about his personal circumstances. Due to its specific treatment of so many situations in life, James is the most practical book in the New Testament, and its timeless principles apply just as well to life today as they did in the first century.

READ JAMES 3

Prayer: *Lord, may I walk in the wisdom from above that is first pure, then peaceable, gentle, reasonable, full of mercy and good fruits, unwavering, without hypocrisy.*

Meditation passage for today: verses 13–18

Day 339—James 4

Selfishness and materialism lead to quarrels, disunity, and pride; James counsels us to humble ourselves and submit to God rather than envying and slandering others (4:1-12). Those who engage in business must submit their plans to God's will and avoid the arrogance of autonomy (4:13-17).

The theme of James is the character of true faith as it is expressed in various situations and relationships. The Jewish believers scattered throughout the Roman Empire were struggling with trials and temptations. There were evidently problems in their assemblies with spiritual apathy, preferential treatment of the wealthy, disunity, and materialism that needed to be corrected. James wrote this letter to exhort them to persevere in obedience to the truth and to apply a living faith in Christ to their attitudes and actions. A lack of change in personal character and conduct is symptomatic of a dead faith.

READ JAMES 4

Prayer: *Lord, may I submit to you in all things and resist the devil. May I draw near to you and humble myself in your presence.*

Meditation passage for today: verses 4, 6-8, 17

Day 340—James 5

Those who depend on their wealth and oppress others will meet with a day of reckoning (5:1-6). Those who are suffering and oppressed must persevere in hope of the promised coming of the Lord (5:7-12). This epistle concludes with a teaching on the healing and restoration that can be accomplished through the prayer offered in faith (5:13-20).

James called himself "a bond-servant of God and of the Lord Jesus Christ" (1:1) and spoke of his readers as brethren whose faith is in "our glorious Lord Jesus Christ" (2:1). While he said less than other New Testament writers about the Person and work of Christ, his words are saturated with allusions to the teaching of our Lord (there are fifteen indirect references in this epistle to the Sermon on the Mount). He anticipated the Lord's coming as the Judge in 5:7-9.

READ JAMES 5

Prayer: *Lord, may I order my steps in accordance with your Word and live in anticipation of the coming of the Lord Jesus. May I be a person of prayer in all circumstances.*

Meditation passage for today: verses 8, 11, 16

Day 341—1 Peter 1

First Peter gives us a divine perspective on living as aliens and strangers in a world that is increasingly hostile to the gospel of Christ. Each of its five chapters alludes to suffering as a very real part of the Christian experience. This letter provides us with counsel and comfort in times of adversity and affliction by pointing us to the living hope we have in our relationship with Christ.

This epistle presents the grace of God in our *salvation* and uses this as the foundation for an attitude of *submission* in the context of *suffering* for Christ's sake. It begins with a portrait of salvation in terms of the believer's future hope of an imperishable inheritance (1:3-5), the joy that is available in spite of present trials (1:6-9), and the predictions of this salvation in the past (1:10-12).

READ 1 PETER 1

Prayer: *Lord, I bless you, the God and Father of our Lord Jesus Christ, who according to your great mercy has caused us to be born again to a living hope through the resurrection of Jesus Christ from the dead, to obtain an imperishable inheritance.*

Meditation passage for today: verses 3-5, 8-9, 13, 22-23

Day 342–1 Peter 2

In view of the gift of salvation, Peter urged believers to grow in holiness and to purify themselves in obedience to the truth (1:13–2:12). As "a chosen race, a royal priesthood, a holy nation, a people for God's own possession" (2:9), they should grow up in their salvation and manifest a new quality of life before a watching world. This gift of salvation is best expressed on a relational level by an attitude of submission and service to others (2:13–3:12). Believers should submit for the Lord's sake to those in government and to those who personally have authority over them (2:13–20). This attitude of submission to God's purposes is best illustrated in the undeserved suffering of Christ (2:21–25), who suffered sinlessly, silently, and as a substitute for others.

READ 1 PETER 2

Prayer: *Lord, may I put aside all malice, deceit, hypocrisy, envy, and slander and long for the pure milk of the Word, so that by it I may grow in respect to salvation.*

Meditation passage for today: verses 1–3, 9, 24–25

Day 343—1 Peter 3

Peter extended this theme of submission to the marital relationship (3:1-7) and to the pursuit of harmonious relationships with others (3:8-12). Submission to the lordship of Christ may lead to suffering for his sake, and Peter encouraged his readers to order their lives in such a way that those who slander them will be ashamed (3:13-17). Peter also pointed to the work of Christ in bringing about their salvation (3:18-22).

The Resurrection transformed the life of Peter, and he played a key role in the formation of the early church and in the spread of the gospel from the Jews to both the Samaritans and the Gentiles. Peter apparently traveled extensively and ministered in various Roman provinces (see 1 Cor 9:5). According to tradition, he was crucified upside down in Rome prior to the death of Nero in A.D. 68, probably sometime in A.D. 64-66.

READ 1 PETER 3

Prayer: *Lord, may I sanctify Christ as Lord in my heart, always being ready to make a defense to everyone who asks me to give an account for the hope that is in me, yet with gentleness and reverence.*

Meditation passage for today: verses 8-9, 15, 18

Day 344—1 Peter 4

Peter urged his readers to live no longer in the lusts of the flesh but in God's power and in service to one another (4:1–11). If they suffer for the sake of Christ, they should commit themselves to the Lord and continue in his service (4:12–19).

First Peter presents a biblical response to suffering in the lives of believers. Peter could anticipate a growing wave of persecution among those who follow Christ, and it appears that he wrote this epistle not long before Christianity was declared to be an illegal religion. He wanted his readers to be prepared to persevere under adversity and not to be surprised at the painful trial they were suffering (4:12). Instead, they should rejoice that they are participating in the sufferings of Christ, because they will exult at the revelation of his glory (4:13).

READ 1 PETER 4

Prayer: *Lord, may I be of sound judgment and sober spirit for the purpose of prayer, and may I keep fervent in my love for others.*

Meditation passage for today: verses 7–13

Day 345—1 Peter 5

Peter exhorted the elders to serve as examples to their flocks and encouraged all his readers to pursue a lifestyle of humility and hope. He reminded his readers that their brethren throughout the world were also undergoing the same kind of sufferings (5:9), and that they were not in a unique situation. Peter wanted to encourage them to submit to God and his loving purposes for their lives and to draw on his strength in the present while maintaining a clear hope of their heavenly future. Thus, the more they realized that they were strangers and aliens in the world, and that their true destiny and home was eternal glory in the presence of the Lord, the better they would be able to stand fast in the true grace of God (5:12).

READ 1 PETER 5

Prayer: *Lord, by your grace may I clothe myself with humility toward others and humble myself under your mighty hand, that you may exalt me at the proper time.*

Meditation passage for today: verses 5–11

Day 346—2 Peter 1

While 1 Peter deals with the problem of external opposition to the gospel, 2 Peter confronts the even more insidious problem of internal opposition to the truth by teachers who profess to be believers but distort the gospel. These false teachers "secretly introduce destructive heresies" (2:1) even to the point of denying Christ, and their teachings seduce believers into error and immorality. This epistle tells us how to deal with the problem of false teaching, which is more relevant in our time of proliferating spiritual counterfeits than ever before.

After a brief salutation (1:1-2), Peter speaks of God's "precious and magnificent promises" and the consequent life of faith, moral excellence, knowledge, self-control, perseverance, godliness, brotherly kindness, and love which these promises should produce (1:3-11). Knowing that his martyrdom was imminent, Peter wanted his readers to remember and hold fast to the prophetic word (1:12-21).

READ 2 PETER 1

Prayer: *Lord, by your grace may I grow in faith, moral excellence, knowledge, self-control, perseverance, godliness, brotherly kindness, and love.*

Meditation passage for today: verses 3-4, 16-19

Day 347—2 Peter 2

Having affirmed true prophecy, Peter warns of the dangers of false teachers who deny the truths of the gospel and seek to captivate others (2:1–22). He not only denounces their teachings and conduct but also anticipates the divine judgment they will receive.

In contrast to the external dangers of persecution of the Christian community in Asia Minor that Peter addressed in his first epistle, his second epistle confronts the internal dangers of false teachers that threatened to corrupt the body of believers in both doctrine and practice. The focus of 1 Peter is *suffering* for the sake of commitment to Christ, while the focus of 2 Peter is *knowledge* of the truth in a context of misleading errors. Peter's first epistle deals with the implications of spiritual *birth*, and his second epistle stresses the importance of spiritual *growth*.

READ 2 PETER 2

Prayer: *Lord, may I come to know the truth of your revealed Word so well that I will be able to quickly discern and avoid the influence of false teaching.*

Meditation passage for today: verses 1, 9

Day 348—2 Peter 3

The promised coming of Christ will happen suddenly and certainly, and Peter refers back to the Creation and the Flood to refute the argument of scoffers who deny that the Day of the Lord will arrive (3:1–10). In view of the fact that the earth and its works will be destroyed, Peter urges his readers to live holy and blameless lives as they look forward to a new heaven and a new earth (3:11–18).

Peter contrasts the destiny of those who are disseminating error and immorality with those who affirm the Scriptures and develop in Christlike character. He exhorts his readers to "grow in the grace and knowledge of our Lord and Savior Jesus Christ" (3:18). Sanctification through application and conformity to scriptural truth is the best defense against spiritual counterfeits. Peter wrote this epistle as a lasting reminder to remain faithful to the foundations of the faith and to urge believers to live holy and godly lives in view of the certain coming of the Lord Jesus.

READ 2 PETER 3

Prayer: *Lord, may I grow in the grace and knowledge of our Lord and Savior Jesus Christ. To him be the glory, both now and to the day of eternity.*

Meditation passage for today: verses 8–14, 18

Day 349—1 John 1

This simple but profound epistle urges us to live out what we profess and to enjoy true fellowship with God by walking in his light, love, and life. It contains a perfect blend of truth and love, firmness and graciousness, exhortation and consolation, warning against false teaching and witness to what is genuine. This powerful little letter both encourages us and challenges us in our faith.

In his prologue, John remembers the apostolic fellowship with Christ and desires to share the joy of that fellowship with his readers (1:1-4). This fellowship is conditioned by walking in the light and is made possible by the blood of Jesus (1:5-10).

READ 1 JOHN 1

Prayer: *Lord, you are Light, and in you there is no darkness at all. When we walk in the Light as you yourself are in the Light, we have fellowship with one another, and the blood of Jesus your Son cleanses us from all sin.*

Meditation passage for today: verses 1-3, 5, 7-9

Day 350—1 John 2

Christ is the believer's Advocate with the Father, and those who know him must do what he commands—love one another (2:1–11). John wanted his readers to grow into maturity in the Word and to overcome the evil one (2:12–14). He cautioned them against the lures of the world system (2:15–17) and against the false teachings of the antichrists who deny that Jesus is the Christ (2:18–27).

First John subtly interweaves and develops various themes such as light, love, life, truth, and righteousness. John made use of several antithetical ideas in this epistle: light and darkness, love and hatred, truth and error, love of the world and love of God's will, righteousness and sin, the children of God and the children of the devil, the Spirit of God and the spirit of the antichrist, life and death. While this is a profound and multilayered epistle, John achieved this with a disarmingly simple vocabulary and style.

READ 1 JOHN 2

Prayer: *Lord, I know that when I sin, I have an Advocate with the Father, Jesus Christ the righteous; and he himself is the propitiation for our sins; and not for ours only, but also for those of the whole world.*

Meditation passage for today: verses 1–2, 15–17, 27–29

Day 351—1 John 3

Not only must we abide in God's light; we must also abide in God's love (2:28–4:21). To do so is to enjoy God's assurance and to practice righteousness, since the practice of sin is incompatible with the believer's new nature (2:28–3:10). When believers sin, they do not reflect the regenerate new person but the works of the devil. Regeneration produces righteousness, and righteousness is expressed in sacrificial love for others (3:11–24).

First John develops the theme of fellowship with God in belief and in practice and argues that belief in Jesus as the Christ becomes evident when it is expressed in actions of love and service of others. John sought to encourage his readers to obey God's command to "believe in the name of his Son Jesus Christ, and love one another, just as he commanded us" (3:23) so that they would enjoy the assurance of Christ's life in them.

READ 1 JOHN 3

Prayer: *Lord, I affirm the greatness of the love you have bestowed on us, that we would be called children of God; and such we are. We know that when Jesus appears, we will be like him, because we will see him just as he is.*

Meditation passage for today: verses 1–3, 11, 16, 18–24

Day 352—1 John 4

Those who have the Spirit of God not only acknowledge the incarnate Christ and the doctrine of the apostles (4:1-6) but also manifest the love of God in their relationships with other believers (4:7-21).

Because of its refutation of gnosticism, 1 John stresses the incarnation of Jesus Christ: "Every spirit that confesses that Jesus Christ has come in the flesh is from God; and every spirit that does not confess Jesus is not from God" (4:2-3). The one who denies that Jesus is the Christ denies both the Father and the Son (2:22). Jesus is the Christ who "came by water and blood" (5:6)–he was the same indivisible Person from his baptism to his crucifixion.

READ 1 JOHN 4

Prayer: *Lord, you manifested your love for us when you sent your only begotten Son into the world so that we might live through him. This is love, not that we loved you but that you loved us and sent your Son to be the propitiation for our sins.*

Meditation passage for today: verses 4, 7–11, 15–18, 21

Day 353—1 John 5

To trust in Jesus as the Christ is to abide in God's life and to enjoy the assurance of eternal life in Christ (5:1–13). "These things I have written to you who believe in the name of the Son of God, so that you may know that you have eternal life" (5:13). This assurance leads to confident access to God in prayer (5:14–17) and the power to overcome the evil one (5:18–21).

John emphasizes the need for belief in Jesus Christ (the Greek word translated "believe" involves personal trust and not merely intellectual assent) and says that this is the condition for the reception of eternal life (3:23; 5:10–13). Jesus Christ, the righteous One, is our Advocate before the Father, and "he himself is the propitiation [satisfaction] for our sins; and not for ours only, but also for those of the whole world" (2:1–2; brackets mine).

READ 1 JOHN 5

Prayer: *Lord, you have given us eternal life, and this life is in your Son. He who has the Son has the life; he who does not have the Son of God does not have the life.*

Meditation passage for today: verses 1–6, 11–14

Day 354—2 John

Second John offers us a brief word of encouragement to continue to walk in God's light by loving and serving one another. It also warns us to be aware of spiritual counterfeits that distort the truth of the gospel of the incarnate Christ. Thus we are to love, but we are also to show discernment; truth without love leads to harshness and severity, while love without truth produces sloppy sentimentality (see "speaking the truth in love," Eph 4:15).

John wrote to encourage his readers not only to hold firm to the apostolic doctrine and practice which "you have heard from the beginning, that you should walk in it" (verse 6) but also to warn them to avoid false teachers and not to take them in or welcome them. They were to love one another in the truth and practice discernment so that they did not fall prey to deceptive influences.

READ 2 JOHN

Prayer: *Lord, may I walk in your truth and obey your commandment to love one another, just as Jesus has loved me.*

Meditation passage for today: verses 3–6

Day 355—3 John

The theme of this epistle is the importance of maintaining fellowship and undergirding the ministries of people who have committed their lives to sharing the message of new life in Christ. John wrote this brief letter to commend Gaius as a fellow worker in the truth because of his hospitality and support of missionaries who had been sent, evidently by John, to teach and equip believers in the churches in the region of Asia Minor. At the same time, this letter rebuked the pride and misconduct of Diotrephes in his rejection of those who taught the truth. John also commended Demetrius (who may have delivered this letter) to the church and informed Gaius of his plan to visit the church and settle the difficulties. The apostle starkly contrasts a man who wants others to look to him and another man who wants others to look to Jesus. One is the embodiment of selfishness and the other of servanthood.

READ 3 JOHN

Prayer: *Lord, may I walk in the truth and rejoice when I see others do the same. May I imitate what is good and avoid what is evil.*

Meditation passage for today: verses 3–4, 11

Day 356—Jude

Jude combined the style of his brother James and the theme of 2 Peter to create a brief but powerful word of warning and exhortation. Many of the New Testament epistles confront the problem of spiritual counterfeits, but Jude is the most passionate in its denunciation of their teachings and practices. This epistle serves as a potent reminder of the reality of the spiritual warfare that is all about us. It teaches us that complacency leads to surrendered territory, while commitment to the Person and cause of Christ will keep us from stumbling.

Although his initial intention was to write "about our common salvation," Jude realized that in view of the growing threat of heretical teachers, he had to urge his readers to "contend earnestly for the faith which was once for all handed down to the saints." Thus, his primary purpose in writing this epistle was to expose the character and tactics of the ungodly deceivers who were infiltrating the churches and seducing believers to follow in their immoral path.

READ JUDE

Prayer: *Lord, to you who are able to keep me from stumbling and to make me stand in the presence of your glory blameless with great joy, to the only God my Savior, through Jesus Christ my Lord, be glory, majesty, dominion, and authority, before all time and now and forever.*

Meditation passage for today: verses 3–4, 20–21, 24–25

Day 357—Revelation 1

Genesis reaches back and portrays the beginning of all things, and Revelation reaches ahead and portrays the consummation of all things in God's judgment of humanity and creation of a new cosmos. This powerful Apocalypse (this word means "unveiling," "disclosure," "revelation") gives us a prophetic look at the completion of God's program and purposes for human history. The book elevates our minds and hearts to the sovereignty, majesty, wisdom, power, holiness, and dominion of the eternal Alpha and Omega.

The Revelation of Jesus Christ begins with a prologue (1:1-3), a salutation that portrays the triune God (1:4-8), and a theophany (a visible manifestation of God) of the omnipotent and omniscient Christ, who will conquer and rule all things (1:9-20).

READ REVELATION 1

Prayer: *Lord, your Son is the faithful witness, the firstborn of the dead, and the ruler of the kings of the earth. He loves us and released us from our sins by his blood, and he has made us to be a kingdom, priests to his God and Father. To him be the glory and the dominion forever and ever.*

Meditation passage for today: verses 4–9, 17–19

Day 358—Revelation 2

Each of the messages to the seven churches in this chapter and the next refers back to an aspect of John's vision of the resurrected Christ and contains a command, a commendation or condemnation, a correction, and a challenge. The seven messages are tailored to the specific needs of these churches, and some expositors have also seen in them a relevance that goes beyond the first-century context. Others see them as portraying some of the general movements in the history of the Christian church.

The rewards for the people of God who "overcome" include eating of the Tree of Life; being unhurt by the second death; receiving a new name and the names of the Father and the Son; gaining the morning star; being clothed in white garments; and sitting with the Lord Jesus on his throne.

READ REVELATION 2

Prayer: *Lord, may I never leave my first love; when I am tempted to pursue lesser lovers, may I look to Jesus and return to him.*

Meditation passage for today: verses 7, 11, 17, 26–28

Day 359—Revelation 3

There are four primary approaches to the interpretation of the Apocalypse: (1) The *symbolic* or *idealist* view argues that this is not a prophetic book but a symbolic portrait of the cosmic conflict of the spiritual forces of good and evil. (2) The *preterist* view (from the Latin word for "past") holds that Revelation symbolically refers to events that took place in the first-century Roman Empire. (3) The *historicist* view interprets Revelation as an allegorical overview of the history of Christendom from its inception to the second advent. (4) The *futurist* view sees the first-century Roman persecution and emperor worship as a type of a far greater conflict that will take place in the future. According to this view, Revelation 6–19 portrays a coming seven-year tribulation that will be terminated by the second advent of Christ.

READ REVELATION 3

Prayer: *Lord, may I always respond to your loving initiatives, and may I be zealous and repent when you reprove and discipline me for my good.*

Meditation passage for today: verses 5, 12, 19–21

Day 360—Revelation 4

The glorious scene in chapters 4–5 brings us into the presence of the triune God. The Father is worshiped as the holy and eternal Creator of all things (4:1–11). The Son is worshiped as the worthy Redeemer who purchased for God with his blood people from every tribe and tongue and people and nation (5:1–10). The Father and the Son together are worshiped in 5:11–14.

Due to its highly symbolic nature, many who have read the Apocalypse have slipped into one extreme of concluding that it is inexplicable and therefore unfruitful to study, or the opposite extreme of speculating about every nuance in the book. It is more profitable to take a middle course: Much of the symbolism of Revelation is explained in the book itself and in other books, such as Ezekiel and Daniel; however, there are a number of things that remain mysterious in Revelation, and we should not be overconfident in supposing that we can decode every part.

READ REVELATION 4

Prayer: *Lord, you are worthy to receive glory and honor and power; for you created all things, and because of your will they existed and were created.*

Meditation passage for today: verses 1–5, 11

Day 361—Revelation 5

G enerally speaking, those who hold the symbolic, preterist, and historicist views are amillennial (Christ's kingdom is taking place now in a spiritual sense) or postmillennial (Christ will return after the church establishes his kingdom by evangelizing society). Those who hold the futurist view are premillennial (there is a spiritual sense in which the kingdom has already come, but after his second advent, Christ will also establish a geopolitical kingdom that will last for a thousand years, and this will be followed by the creation of a new heaven and a new earth).

Thus, our understanding of John's purpose in writing the Revelation depends on which interpretive approach we take. However, all would agree that one purpose of this book was to encourage its recipients in a time of persecution by assuring them of God's ultimate triumph over the forces of evil. It was also written to challenge them to persevere and to hold fast to the truth, because God will reward those who love his Son.

READ REVELATION 5

Prayer: *Lord, worthy is the Lamb that was slain to receive power and riches and wisdom and might and honor and glory and blessing.*

Meditation passage for today: verses 5–6, 9, 12–14

Day 362—Revelation 19

Chapters 6–18 portray a time of earthly tribulation and heavenly conflict that centers around three cycles of seven judgments: seven seals (6:1–8:5), seven trumpets (8:6–11:1), and seven bowls (15:1–19:6). There are prophetic inserts between the sixth and seventh seal and trumpet judgments, as well as a lengthy supplement between the trumpet and bowl judgments. In addition, chapters 17–18 describe the overthrow of "the great harlot" and of Babylon the Great.

After the three cycles of judgment and the wedding supper of the Lamb, the Lord Jesus Christ returns to the earth in power and glory to overthrow the Beast and the kings of the earth (chapter 19). Jesus comes in majesty to reign over the earth as the King of Kings and Lord of Lords.

READ REVELATION 19

Prayer: *Lord, blessed are those who are invited to the marriage supper of the Lamb. He is the Word of God, the King of Kings, and the Lord of Lords.*

Meditation passage for today: verses 6–9, 11–16

Day 363—Revelation 20

In this chapter, the Lord confines Satan, reigns on the earth for a "thousand years" (verses 2–6), defeats Satan and his forces in a final conflict, and judges the dead. Those who are a part of the first resurrection will not be touched by the second (spiritual) death, but those whose names are not written in the Book of Life will be judged at the great white throne and cast into the lake of fire.

Revelation blends apocalyptic, prophetic, and epistolary literature into a unique whole that uses ecstatic visions, admonitions, figurative language, graphic images of worldwide judgments, and sublime renderings of God's glorious character and reign. There are many parallels between the beginning in the first three chapters of Genesis and the new beginning in the last three chapters of Revelation.

READ REVELATION 20

Prayer: *Lord, I know that an hour is coming when the dead will hear the voice of the Son of God, and those who hear will live. For just as the Father has life in himself, even so he gave to the Son to have life in himself; and he gave him authority to execute judgment, because he is the Son of Man.*

Meditation passage for today: verses 4–6

Day 364—Revelation 21

A new heaven and earth is created, this time unspoiled by sin, death, pain, or sorrow. The New Jerusalem (described in 21:9–22:5) is shaped like a gigantic cube, fifteen hundred miles in length, width, and height (the most holy place in the Old Testament tabernacle and temple was also a perfect cube). Its multicolored stones will reflect the glory of God, and it will continually be filled with light. The greatest thing of all is that believers will be in the presence of God, and "they will see his face" (22:4).

The Apocalypse has been given an appropriate place as the last book in the canon of Scripture because it ties the themes of the Bible together. In a very real sense, chapters 21–22 are the new Genesis but without the Fall. In broadest terms, the Bible conveys the metanarrative of God's work in creation, redemption, and re-creation, and this story centers on the incarnation of the God-man.

READ REVELATION 21

Prayer: *Lord, thank you that in the new heaven and new earth, you will dwell among us, and we will be your people. You will wipe away every tear from our eyes, and there will no longer be any death; there will no longer be any mourning, or crying, or pain; the first things will pass away.*

Meditation passage for today: verses 1–7, 22–27

Day 365—Revelation 22

Revelation concludes with an epilogue that assures the readers that the Lord will come soon (22:6–21). Jesus Christ is portrayed in Revelation as the sovereign Ruler and Judge, and his might, majesty, power, and dominion are seen throughout this book. The titles ascribed to him in the Apocalypse include the faithful Witness, the Firstborn of the dead, the Ruler of the kings of the earth (1:5); the first and the last (1:17); the living One (1:18); the Son of God (2:18); he who is holy, who is true, who has the key of David (3:7); the Amen, the faithful and true Witness, the Beginning of the creation of God (3:14); the Lion that is from the tribe of Judah, the Root of David (5:5); the Lamb (5:6 and following); Faithful and True (19:11); The Word of God (19:13); King of Kings and Lord of Lords (19:16); the Alpha and the Omega, the beginning and the end (22:13); the descendant of David, the bright Morning Star (22:16); and the Lord Jesus (22:21).

READ REVELATION 22

Prayer: *Lord, your Son is coming quickly, and his reward is with him; he is the Alpha and the Omega, the first and the last, the beginning and the end. Come, Lord Jesus.*

Meditation passage for today: verses 3–7, 12–13, 16–17, 20

About the Authors

Kenneth Boa is engaged in a ministry of relational evangelism and discipleship, teaching, writing, and speaking. He holds a B.S. from Case Institute of Technology, a Th.M. from Dallas Theological Seminary, a Ph.D. from New York University, and a D.Phil. from the University of Oxford in England.

Dr. Boa is the President of Reflections Ministries, an organization that seeks to provide safe places for people to consider the claims of Christ and to help them mature and bear fruit in their relationship with God. He is also President of Trinity House Publishers, a publishing company that is dedicated to the creation of tools that will help people manifest eternal values in a temporal arena by drawing them to intimacy with God and a better understanding of the culture in which they live.

Recent publications by Dr. Boa include *Faith Has It's Reasons, Conformed to His Image, An Unchanging Faith in a Changing World; Face to Face; Pursing Wisdom; The Art of Living Well; Wisdom at Work, Living What You Believe,* and *Sacred Readings.* He is a contributing editor to *The Open Bible,* the *Promise Keeper's Men's Study Bible, The Leadership Bible,* the consulting editor of the *Zondervan NASB Study Bible,* and the Editor-in-Chief of *The Life Promises Bible.*

Karen Boa has a B.A. from Montclair State University in English and has done graduate work at New York University in comparative literature. She continues to develop her interests in literature, film, music, and art, and she is an avid gardener.

Kenneth Boa writes a free monthly teaching letter called "Reflections." If you would like to be on the mailing list, call 800-DRAW NEAR (800-372-9632).